Silvia
London
Oct. 96.

Insurance

Unit 1-10

Professional Reading Skills Series

Accounting M Sneyd
Advertising and the Promotion Industry M J St John
International Banking and Finance M Sneyd
Marketing M J St John
Tourism N McBurney

English for Academic Purposes Series

Agriculture C St J Yates
Business Studies C Vaughan James
Computer Science T Walker
Earth Sciences C St J Yates
Economics C St J Yates
General Engineering D & C M Johnson
Medicine D V James

Other titles of interest

Business Management English: Finance J Comfort & N Brieger
Business Management English: Language Reference for Business English N Brieger & J Comfort
Business Management English: Marketing J Comfort & N Brieger
Business Management English: Personnel N Brieger & J Comfort
Business Management English: Production and Operations N Brieger & J Comfort

Professional Reading Skills Series

INSURANCE

Michael R Sneyd

Prentice Hall

New York London Toronto Sydney Tokyo Singapore

PRENTICE HALL INTERNATIONAL ENGLISH LANGUAGE TEACHING

First published 1996 by
Prentice Hall International
Campus 400, Spring way
Maylands Avenue, Hemel Hempstead
Hertfordshire, HP2 7EZ

Printed and bound in Great Britain by
Redwood Books, Trowbridge, Wiltshire

Library of Congress Cataloging-in-Publication Data

Sneyd. Michael R.
Insurance / Michael R. Sneyd.
p. cm. — (Professional reading skills series)
ISBN 0-13-017740-7 (pbk.)
1. Insurance. 2. Readers — Insurance. I Title. II Series.
HG8051.S597 1996
368 — dc20 95-40083
CIP

British Library Cataloguing in Publication Data

A catalogue record for this book is available from the British Library

ISBN 0-13-017740-7

5 4 3 2 1
1999 98 97 96

Contents

* These texts do not appear on the cassette

Acknowledgements

The texts in this book appear with the permission of those who hold the copyright. The author and publisher thank the following for permission to reproduce copyright material:

Prentice Hall for extracts from *Introduction to Insurance*; Woodhead Faulkner for extracts from *What Goes on in Insurance* and *An Introduction to Risk Management*; John Wiley and Sons Inc. for extracts from *Principles and Practice of Insurance* and *Fundamentals of Risk and Insurance*; Ewan MacNaughton Associates for extracts from *The Daily Telegraph*; Macmillan for extract from *Macmillan Family Encyclopaedia* and from *Marketing*; Royal Insurance plc for their leaflet; *The Financial Times* for extracts; *The Economist* for extracts; Oxford University Press for definitions from *The Oxford Dictionary of Business English*; Longman for definitions from *The Longman Dictionary of Contemporary English*; the Credit Insurance Association Ltd for extracts from *A Credit to the Company.*

Every effort has been made to obtain copyright permission. The publisher will be glad to make suitable arrangements with copyright holders whom it has not been possible to contact.

Introduction

General information

English is often used in specialist journals, books and magazines to reach an international public. This book is one of a series which is designed to develop your reading skills and improve your familiarity with how English is used in particular professional areas of work.

The book contains texts, exercises and an answer key. It is accompanied by a cassette so that you can also listen to the reading texts being read aloud.

Using the book

The units
Each unit of the book contains one or more texts and a range of activities. These become more difficult so you will probably benefit most from working through the units in order. However, it is possible to use the units in any order. To help you see links and relationships, reference is sometimes made to a similar activity in a previous unit; you do not need to have done that activity but it may help you if you have.

Reading techniques
Before reading a text we suggest that you think about the topic; there are often pre-reading questions to help you do this. Then practise the techniques of skimming and scanning: skimming involves quickly finding the main ideas, usually by looking at the first and last paragraphs and the first sentences of other paragraphs; scanning is looking through the text for particular information, usually looking for key words, dates, numbers, etc., that is, information which can be found by running your eye up and down the page rather than along each line. Skim and scan questions are given before the text. All this prepares you for understanding the details of the text, extracting information from it and answering specific questions.

Using the cassette

Why listen?
The texts are read aloud by a native speaker of English so that you can relate the sound of the spoken word to the written word. English is not always pronounced as it is spelt and so it can be difficult to recognise, in conversation, words you have learnt through reading and vice versa. Also, there is evidence that suggests that our brains store words according to how they sound, so if you know how they sound you may remember and recall them more easily. Hearing a text while following the written version can also improve comprehension.

What to listen for
Listen for groups of words and think about why they are grouped together. Notice the pauses and changes of tone in the voice; these can help you to identify different ideas and parts of the text and to recognise the transition from one part to the next. The stress given to words can also be an indication of their importance.

When to listen
It is often useful to listen to the cassette recording of the text after skimming and scanning and before a closer reading. At this stage, listen to the recording just once while you follow the text in the book. Then do the activities. After completing the exercises, you may like to listen to the recording several times, both with the text in front of you and without it.

The texts

Sources
The texts are taken from a range of recent publications such as books, magazines and newspapers. They have not been written for language learning but for people in professional fields to communicate with each other. They have been selected to cover a range of topics but also to show different kinds of writing. In some texts, the language is quite formal; in others it is more like speech and contains a lot of casual (colloquial) expressions, and you may only need to understand the general meaning of these.

Some of the texts were written and published in the United States and use American spelling. This should not affect you when reading, but when you write you should be consistent and either always use American spelling or always use British spelling.

Text types
The information, the order in which it occurs and the type of language depend on who the texts were written for (the audience) and why the text was written (the purpose). Texts will vary according to whether they are written for students, specialists or the general public and whether the intention is to explain, advertise, persuade, etc. As well as the information and the order in which it is presented, the choice of language and words will depend on the audience and the purpose. Thinking about these issues when you first meet a text can help you to understand it better.

The exercises

These are divided into five main categories: the first two are presented before the text. The questions that come after the text require you to read more carefully and will help you understand the information and learn more about the language. It is important to be able to explain how you reached an answer and what part(s) of the text you used as this shows deep, rather than surface, understanding.

In the main, there are three kinds of activities after the text. Not every text has questions of each kind or the same number of questions. The exercises reflect the type of text and the language and meaning in it. So, for instance, one text may have lots of

Vocabulary questions but no Text Organisation ones. However, in each unit you will find there is a range of activities. The usual order is Text Organisation, Comprehension, Vocabulary. This is because you should learn to see the text as a whole message rather than as a series of words.

Pre-reading

The first text in each unit is always preceded by pre-reading questions. These are designed to set you thinking about the particular topic because this will help you to understand the text. Some but not all of the other texts have pre-reading questions, too. If you have already read one or more texts you will already be thinking and focusing on the topic and so extra questions may not be necessary.

Skimming and scanning

As already mentioned, when we have a text to read it is often helpful and time-saving to skim read it first; that is, glance at it very quickly just to get an overall idea of what the text is about. At other times, we only want to extract some specific information from the text and so we just scan; that is, look very quickly for words associated with our information. These are techniques which are useful when reading in any language and which improve with practice. Before most texts you will find two or three skim and scan questions and you should aim to find the answers in just a few seconds.

Text organisation

These questions are to help you see how the writer has organised the information. There are certain patterns and conventions which develop the structure of the text and it is easier to understand the detailed information if you can follow the general way in which it is organised. This can also help you to see ways to organise your own writing.This is a good point at which to think about the audience and purpose.

Comprehension questions

These are to help you to understand the important information and, often, to record it in note form using tables, lists, etc. Some questions can be answered by looking at just one part of the text; to answer others you will have to select and relate information from different parts of the text. You may be asked to write short answers, to underline information in the text, to decide if statements are true or false, to match, to order, to complete lists, charts or tables or to fill in gaps, etc. Where the exercise requires you to fill in a table or gaps, a standard size space has been left; the size of the space or length of the gap does not indicate the number or length of the missing word(s), unless otherwise stated.

Vocabulary questions

These are aimed to help you understand the texts more fully as well as to help you to acquire a wider vocabulary. Specialised words are marked with an asterisk (*) and their meaning can be found in the glossary at the back of this book. In addition, it is important that you become sensitive to whether words are formal or informal so that you can use them in the correct context, and this aspect is practised. The concept of metaphor is also introduced and worked with. Metaphor is very much a feature of journalistic writing and is therefore vital to anyone who wishes to read newspapers and magazines. Some questions deal with the meaning of individual words but most deal with words in relation to each other. Learning isolated words can make it difficult to know how to use them. If you learn words as phrases and sets of related items then you will find it easier to remember and use them. One sort of vocabulary activity involves collocations and word partnerships: many words are used in fairly specific combinations or partnerships. You will find it easier and more useful to remember partnerships rather than individual words.

In some units there are other types of questions under the heading 'Viewpoints'. These may ask you about the author's or your view of a topic.

Answer key

As the activities have been carefully designed to help you learn as much as possible about the language and the topic, the answers are important. You should think about them carefully and think about *how* you reached your answer. The actual answer applies only to that text. The process by which you reached your answer can be applied to many texts and so there is more to be learnt from that.

The answer key does not usually contain answers to the pre-reading questions as they are to do with your knowledge and opinion rather than particular facts. Where there is only one factual answer this is given.

Where you are asked to write words or expressions and fill in gaps there is often more than one suitable answer. Those in the answer key should be seen as representative only; others of similar meaning would be equally acceptable. It is understanding the texts and learning from them that is important, not using exactly the same words as are suggested in the answer key.

Using these books in class

In a class you can benefit from working on the exercises with a partner or in a small group of three or four. The discussion that results helps you to learn, especially if you have to explain your answer and how you reached it. When a question is causing difficulties, working in a small group means you can help each other and work towards a suitable answer. This helps you to become less dependent on the teacher.

Unit 1 The basis of insurance

In this unit there are two texts about ideas which are essential to the operation of insurance. The first text gives a description of how insurance works financially. The second text looks at three fundamental legal principles of insurance.

Text 1.1 A financial definition of insurance

Pre-reading

Why do you think insurance developed? How would our lives be different today if there was no insurance available?

Skim and scan

(a) Is the style of writing in this text formal or informal?

(b) From which of the following do you think this text was taken?

(i) a newspaper
(ii) a children's book
(iii) a textbook
(iv) an advertising brochure

Note: All words in a text preceded by an asterisk (*) can be found in the glossary at the back of this book.

A financial definition of insurance

1 Throughout human history, unexpected economic losses have occurred. Such losses would continue to occur whether or not a system of insurance had ever been devised. But through the operation of an insurance system, losses can be predicted before they occur. The predictability of losses in advance is basic to an insurance system's operations. Because an insurance system allows losses to be predicted in advance, it allows the cost of losses to be financed and redistributed in advance.

2 The first definition of insurance that we will examine is the financial one. In this instance, *insurance is a financial arrangement that redistributes the costs of unexpected losses.* The insurance arrangement involves the transfer of many different exposures to loss to one insurance pool, which combines the numerous exposures.

3 An insurance system accomplishes the redistribution of the costs of losses by collecting a premium payment from every participant in the system. In exchange for the payment of the premium, the insured receives a promise from the insurance system to be compensated in the event of a loss. In most insurance systems only a small percentage of those insured suffer losses. Thus, an insurance system redistributes the costs of losses from the unfortunate few

members who experience them to *all* the members of the insurance pool (including those who suffer losses) who have paid premiums.

4 Diagram 1 illustrates the way in which a fire insurance pool redistributes the costs of losses. Assume that each member of the pool is exposed to loss of his home by fire. Each member willingly contributed a premium – $800 – to the insurance pool in exchange for the promise of payment in the event of fire. Assume that homeowner # 4644 loses his house in a fire. He will collect $100,000, the insured value of his house, from the insurance pool. If there were no insurance pool, the unfortunate victim would lose $100,000. But instead, all the members of the pool have each paid $800 to provide funds to pay for losses. Thus, each insured has paid a part of the $100,000 loss experienced by one member.

Diagram 1: Insurance redistributes the costs of losses

You will fill in the spaces A–H for Exercise 2, page 3.

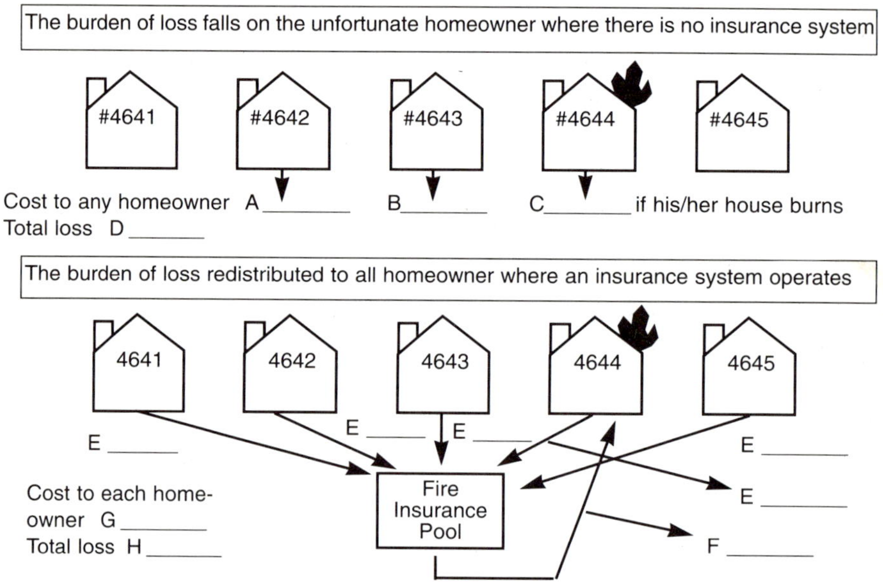

5 The $800 premium each insured paid in advance was calculated from the losses predicted by the insurance system. When the year began it was not predicted that home # 4644 would burn but, rather, that 33 houses from among the 5,000 insured would burn. From this prediction came the decision to charge each homeowner $800 for his or her insurance.

6 An insurance system is able to operate because all the *insureds are willing to substitute a relatively small certain outlay, the insurance premium, for a relatively large uncertain loss. It is generally assumed that most people find the possibility of suffering a large loss unpleasant to contemplate. Therefore, people are willing to pay an insurance premium to be relieved of the uncertainty about a loss, as well as to be compensated if the loss actually occurs. Thus, even if no loss occurs during a year, as will be the case for most insureds, value has still been received in the form of a reduced or eliminated unpleasant mental state, the anxiety about a loss.

'Introduction to Insurance', Dorfman, Mark S. (3rd edn, Prentice Hall, 1987)

* person or organization which is covered by a particular insurance policy

When doing the exercises below do not worry about individual words you do not understand. Do not use a dictionary. You will see that you can do the exercises without understanding every word.

Text organisation

1. There are six paragraphs in the text. Match each paragraph with one of the headings below. The first one has been done for you.

Heading	Paragraph number
(i) Losses are shared by insurance.	3
(ii) Premiums are based on prediction.	
(iii) How an insurance pool works.	
(iv) Insurance is defined financially.	
(v) Insurance provides peace of mind.	
(vi) Future losses can be predicted.	

Comprehension

2. The following amounts are missing from Diagram 1:

$800 $100,000 $0

Decide in which space in the diagram they should go. Some amounts must be used more than once.

Space in Diagram 1	Amount
(i) Space A	
(ii) Space B	
(iii) Space C	
(iv) Space D	
(v) Space E	
(vi) Space F	
(vii) Space G	
(viii) Space H	

3. Say whether the following statements are true or false according to the text. Identify the paragraphs in which you find the answers.

Statement	True/false	Paragraph number
(i) Insurance has stopped economic losses from happening.		
(ii) Insurance is only possible because losses can be predicted.		
(iii) An insurance system means that the cost of losses is limited to a few people.		
(iv) An insured person only benefits from his insurance when he suffers a loss.		

4. Using each of the words below once only, complete the following paragraph so that it is correct according to the text.

compensation	exposure	pool	redistribution	premium

The ____________ is the sum of money which each individual in an insurance scheme pays into the ____________ . As a result of paying this, the individual protects himself against ____________ to loss and he receives ____________ if he does have a loss. In this way there is a(n) ____________ of an individual's loss among all the scheme's members.

5. (a) What do these figures represent in the text?
   (i) 33 (ii) 5,000

   (b) In the example shown in Diagram 1 and discussed in paragraphs 4 and 5, why does each householder have to pay $800 insurance?

Vocabulary

6. When reading a text in a foreign language, readers tend to worry too much about understanding every single word. This is often not necessary if you only want to understand the general sense of a passage. Also it is often possible to guess the meaning of a new word in a text by looking at the context of that word. So for the next exercise pay careful attention to the contexts of the words below and work out their meanings. These words are all important in the field of insurance.

   (a) In lines 7 and 18 'redistributes' means:
   (i) adds to
   (ii) reduces
   (iii) spreads
   (iv) stops

   (b) In lines 11 and 12 'exposures to' means:
   (i) experiences of
   (ii) possibilities of
   (iii) results of
   (iv) reasons for

   (c) In lines 11, 19, 21, etc. 'pool' means:
   (i) total amount collected
   (ii) total amount paid for losses
   (iii) total number of members
   (iv) total value of insured property

   (d) In lines 14, 15, 20, etc. 'premium' means:
   (i) a bonus received by each insured person
   (ii) an extra payment by an insured person who suffers loss
   (iii) an amount paid by some insured persons only
   (iv) cost of insurance to an individual

(e) In lines 16 and 40 'to be compensated' means:
  (i) to receive a request for further payment
  (ii) to receive payment for any loss suffered
  (iii) to receive more money than the loss suffered
  (iv) to receive a demand to pay higher premiums

Text 1.2 Legal principles of insurance

Skim and scan

Read this text quickly and decide which of the three headings, A, B or C, the titles below correspond to. You don't need to understand the words used in these titles to do this.

(i) Indemnity
(ii) Insurable interest
(iii) Utmost good faith

Legal principles of insurance

• **HEADING A**

1 It is sometimes said that insurance is like gambling. In betting, for example, one gives a sum of money to a bookmaker who agrees to pay out on the bet if the horse one has backed wins the race. The law however has found a means of distinguishing between gambling contracts, which it will not enforce, and insurance contracts, which it will. For a contract to be one of insurance the insured person must have an insurable interest in the subject matter of the insurance. That is, he must stand to lose financially if the event insured against happens. In life insurance, for example, a man or woman obviously has an interest in his or her own life and can therefore insure it and also the life of a husband or wife. But one cannot insure the life of anybody else unless their death would result in financial loss to oneself. Similarly, with property, insurance may only be effected if one stands to lose financially by its loss or destruction. Clearly the owner of the property would lose but so also might other people, such as a *building society which has lent money on the security of a house or a dry cleaner who has taken in clothes for cleaning.

• **HEADING B**

2 Further, in insurances on property or against liabilities the law applies the principle that the *policyholder must not make a profit if the event insured against happens. The insurance contract is said to be one of indemnity, to make good the insured's loss and no more. Suppose, for example, that property is insured for more than its value and is destroyed as a result of an event insured against. The insured's recovery will be limited to the actual value. Again, if the property has been insured twice over and is destroyed, the insured will not be entitled to recover in all more than its total value. And if insured property is

destroyed in circumstances which give the insured a right to claim both against his own insurer and against some other person who was responsible for the damage, the insured must allow the insurer to have the benefit of the right to claim against the other person.

- **HEADING C**

3 Contracts of insurance form a special class of contract in that the law requires both parties to them, the insured and the insurer, to exercise the utmost good faith towards each other. In particular when anyone applies for insurance (he is known as the proposer) he must tell the prospective insurer every fact that he knows or ought to know which would influence a prudent insurer in deciding whether to grant the insurance and, if so, on what terms. To take an example, a proposer for life insurance must reveal if he has recently had a heart attack as this may be a sign that he is more likely to die prematurely. Similarly if a motorist is seeking to insure his car and has had a number of recent road accidents he must reveal that fact so that the insurer can decide whether to charge him an above-normal premium because he appears to be especially prone to accidents. If any fact of the kind described is not disclosed by the proposer, or if any fact is misstated, even unintentionally, the insurer is entitled to refuse to pay a claim under the policy. Insurers maintain that this is only right because the proposer knows the facts and the insurer does not. The insurer needs to be put in a fair position to decide whether to accept an insurance and on what terms.

'What Goes on in Insurance?', Cockerell, H.A.L.,(Woodhead-Faulkner, 1982)

Text organisation

1. In pieces of writing, pronouns (e.g. 'it', 'them', 'those' etc.) are used to refer to something mentioned earlier in the piece or to something which will be mentioned later. Understanding what pronouns are referring to in any kind of writing is very important for seeing the logical structure. To practise this skill, find out what the following pronouns in 'Legal principles' refer to. Give line references for your answers. The first one has been done for you. (Remember, pronouns can refer forwards as well as backwards.)

Pronoun	Refers to	Line number
(i) It (line 1)	that insurance is like gambling.	1
(ii) it (line 4)	the law	3
(iii) it (Line 5)	the law	3
(iv) one (line 5)	a contract 5	
(v) it (line 9)	his/her own life.	
(vi) its (line 12) 11	property	
(vii) its (line 21) 20	property	
(viii) them (line 30) 29	contracts of insurance	
(ix) he (lines 31 and 32)	anyone who applies for insurance	
(x) this (line 36) 35	if he has recently had a heart attack	34
(xi) this (line 42) 41	the previous sentence	

Comprehension

2. Put the statements (i)–(vi) into the chart according to the heading they refer to. Identify the lines in the text where you find the answer. The first one has been done for you.

Insurable interest	Indemnity	Utmost good faith
(iv) l 10-13	(ii) l 16-19	(i) (lines ~~35–39~~) 30-33
(vi) l 13-15	(v) 21-23	(iii) l 39-41

(i) This principle demands complete honesty when agreeing insurance.
(ii) This principle prevents an insurance loss producing a profit.
(iii) This principle does not accept forgetfulness as an excuse.
(iv) This principle ensures that only those who have suffered loss benefit.
(v) This principle prevents a person from claiming insurance twice for one loss.
(vi) This principle allows people other than the owner of some property to be compensated for its loss.

3. Look at the following cases of insurance claims. From what is said in the text, decide if the insurance company must pay the insurance claim in each case. Tick (✓) the box on the right if the company has to pay. Put a cross (**x**) if it doesn't have to pay.

	Insurance claim	Insurance company must pay?
(a)	A man who was found guilty of dangerous driving changes his insurance company. He buys a new car but does not tell his new insurance company about his previous convictions. He has an accident. He claims from his insurance company.	x
(b)	An old woman's daughter dies. The daughter has been supporting her mother financially. The mother claims on her daughter's life insurance policy.	✓
(c)	A woman buys a house worth £70,000. She insures it for £100,000. The house burns down and she claims £100,000 from her insurer.	x
(d)	A man's car is badly damaged in a crash. The crash was the other driver's fault. The man receives full payment from the guilty driver's insurance company. He then claims from his own insurance for the damage to his car.	x
(e)	A person states on his life insurance application form that his father and grandfather died from lung cancer. He himself is a heavy smoker and also dies from lung cancer. His wife claims from the insurance company.	✓

Vocabulary

4. Although you should not use a dictionary too soon when you try to read something it is, of course, important to be able to use a dictionary effectively and quickly. To improve this skill, use the dictionary definitions below to work out the meanings of these words as they occur in the text.

(i) effected (line 14)
(ii) liabilities (line 19)
(iii) indemnity (line 22)
(iv) to grant (line 39)
(v) proposer (line 40)
(vi) prone (line 45)

effect[1] /ɪˈfekt/ *n* [C;U (on, upon)] **1** a result or condition produced by a cause; something that happens when one thing acts on another: *One of the effects of this illness is that you lose your hair. / suffering from the effects of too much alcohol / The advertising campaign didn't have much effect on sales. / The disclosures had the effect of reducing the government's popularity.* **2** a result produced on the mind or feelings; an IMPRESSION: *Her new red dress produced quite an effect on everyone. Don't look at the details, consider the general effect. / Don't pay any attention to him – he's only doing it* **for effect.** (= to shock or surprise people) **3 in effect:** a in operation: *The old system of taxation will remain in effect until next May.* **b** in fact, although perhaps not appearing so: *Their response was in effect a refusal.* –see also EFFECTIVELY (2) **4 into effect** into operation: *a new system of taxation will come/be brought/be put into effect next May.* **5 take effect**: a to come into operation: *The new system will take effect next May.* **b** to begin to produce results: *The medicine quickly took effect.* **6 to ... effect** *fml* with (the stated) general meaning or result: *He called me a fool,* or words to that effect. | *She has made an announcement* to the effect that *more people will lose their jobs.* | *These weapons were first used, to devastating effect* (= with very destructive results), *in 1945.* –see also EFFECTS, GREENHOUSE EFFECT, SIDE EFFECT; see AFFECT (USAGE)
effect[2] *v* [T] *fml* to cause; produce: *We have tried our best to effect a reconciliation between the two parties.* SEE AFFECT (USAGE)

li-a-bil-i-ty /laɪəˈbɪləti/ n **1** [U (**for, to**)] the condition of being liable: *The new law exempts them from all liability in these matters. / Taking extra vitamins may reduce your liability to colds.* **2** [C] something for which one is responsible, esp. by law: *A child is its parents' liability.* **3** [C] also **liabilities** *pl.* – *tech* the amount of debt that must be paid: *If your liabilities exceed your assets, you may go bankrupt.* – compare ASSET (1); see also LIMITED LIABILITY **4** [C] *infml* someone or something that limits one's activities or freedom: *This old car's a real liability; I can't use it but I have to pay for somewhere to keep it.* – compare ASSET (2)

indemnify *verb* (finance/commerce)
1 to repay someone for money spent or goods lost or damaged: *You will be indemnified for costs incurred on the company's behalf.*
2 to promise to protect someone from money lost or goods damaged: *The water companies were indemnified by the government against legal action.*

/ɪnˈdemnɪfaɪ/
indemnify, indemnifying, indemnified
note transitive verb
⋈ **indemnify** someone *for* something: **indemnify** someone *against* something
▶ **guarantee² 2**

---

indemnity *noun* (finance/commerce)
a promise to protect someone from money lost or goods damaged; repayment for this. An insurance contract that promises to pay for the replacement or repair of lost or damaged goods is a form of indemnity: *arrange an indemnity against loss demand an indemnity for the delayed payment | The courts have allowed the company directors to seek indemnity following the unwelcome takeover.*

/ɪnˈdemnəti/
pl indemnities
⋈ an **indemnity** agreement, arrangement
▶ **compensation, cover¹ 3, guarantee¹ 2, insurance, letter of indemnity**

grant¹ /grɑːnt ‖ grænt/ *v* [T] **1** *fml* to agree to fulfil or allow to be fulfilled: *They granted her request.* | *At last my wish was granted.* (= what I wished for happened) **2** *fml* to give, esp. as a favour: *In response to the lawyer's appeals, the Home Secretary granted a free pardon.* [+ *obj(i)+obj(d)*] *The country was granted its independence in 1961.* | *They have been granted permission to pull down the old theatre.* **3** to admit the truth of (something) to (someone): *I had to grant the logic of his argument.* [+ *obj + (that)*] *I grant you (that) the government isn't very popular at the moment, but I still think it will win the next election* **4 granted** yes (but): *"We were very successful last year." "Granted. But can we do it again this year?"* **5 granted that** (in an argument) even though; even supposing that: *Granted that he should send money to help with the bills, it doesn't mean he will.* **6 take something/someone for granted: a** to accept a fact or situation without questioning its rightness: *I took it for granted that you'd want to come with us, so I bought you a ticket.* **b** to treat someone or something with too little attention or concern; not recognize the true value of: *He's so busy with his job that he takes his family for granted.*

proposal INSCE. a printed form filled in and handed to an insurer by a *proposer,* a person intending to effect an insurance. The form gives the insurer the information he needs so that he can decide whether to accept the proposed insurance, and if so, what rate of premium to charge. The form is usu. a list of questions with spaces for writing the answers.
proposer (1) INSCE. *see* proposal. (2) MAN at a formal meeting, the person who formally puts a motion to the meeting. He has the right to speak first in any discussion of that motion and to speak again at the end, immediately before a vote is taken. *See also* seconder.

prone /prəʊn/ *adj* **1** [F + *to-v*/**to**] likely to suffer (usu. something undesirable): *People are more prone to make mistakes when they are tired.* | *Women are especially prone to this disease.* | *strike-prone industries* | *Mary's always hurting herself; she's very* **accident-prone**. **2** *fml* lying on one's front, face downwards: *They stepped over his prone body.* – compare PROSTRATE, SUPINE (1) – **~ness** *n* [U **(to)**]

5. For each of the words below, choose the meaning which is closest to how the word is used in the text. If you are not sure about the meaning from the context, use a dictionary.
   (a) In line 4 'enforce' means:
      (i) provide
      (ii) attack
      (iii) apply
      (iv) defend
   (b) In line 30 'exercise' means:
      (i) promise
      (ii) show
      (iii) propose
      (iv) ensure
   (c) In line 30 'utmost' means:
      (i) greatest
      (ii) least
      (iii) average amount of
      (iv) unchanging
   (d) In line 32 'prospective' means:
      (i) future
      (ii) possible
      (iii) certain
      (iv) present
   (e) In line 33 'prudent' means:
      (i) well-off
      (ii) suspicious
      (iii) unsuspecting
      (iv) careful

6. Different forms of the word 'insure' are used in the text. Look at how each one is used and then write it below under the heading 'Noun' or 'Adjective'. The numbers next to the headings show how many different forms of the word 'insure' you should find in the text.

Noun (3)	Adjective (3)
INSURANCE INSURED INSURER	INSURED INSURABLE INSURANCE

Viewpoint

Do you think some kinds of insurance should be compulsory for everyone? If you think so, which ones would you make compulsory? Why?

Unit 2 Life and health insurance

In this unit the first text examines the ways in which life insurance is different from other kinds of insurance. The second text discusses how private health insurance in Britain might develop in the future compared to the situation now.

Text 2.1 Some unique characteristics of life insurance

Pre-reading

Can you suggest how life insurance is different from other types of insurance? How do you think insurance companies calculate the value of a human life?

Skim and scan

(a) Which of these three important insurance principles does the text *not* discuss: insurable interest, utmost good faith or indemnity?

(b) What is it *not* possible for insurance to do in relation to a human life?

Some unique characteristics of life insurance

1 Life insurance is a *risk-pooling plan, an economic device through which the risk of premature death is transferred from the individual to the group. However, the contingency insured against has certain characteristics that make it unique; as a result, the contract insuring against the contingency is different in many respects from other types of insurance. The event insured against is an eventual certainty. No one lives forever. Yet life insurance does not violate the requirements of an insurable risk, for it is not the possibility of death itself that is insured, but rather untimely death. The risk in life insurance is not whether the individual is going to die, but when, and the risk increases from year to year. The chance of loss under a life insurance contract is greater the second year of the contract, as far as the company is concerned, than it was the first year, and so on, until the insured eventually dies. Yet, through the mechanism of the *law of large numbers, as we shall see, the insurance company can promise to pay a specified sum to the beneficiary no matter when death comes.

2 There is no possibility of partial loss in life insurance as there is in the case of property and liability insurance. Therefore, all policies are cash payment policies. In the event that a loss occurs, the company will pay the face amount of the policy.

Life insurance is not a contract of indemnity

3 The principle of indemnity applies on a modified basis in the case of life insurance. In most lines of insurance, an attempt is made to put the individual back in exactly the same financial position after a loss as before the loss. For obvious reasons, this is not possible in life insurance. The simple fact of the matter is that we cannot place a value on a human life.

4 As a legal principle, every contract of insurance must be supported by an insurable interest, but in life insurance, the requirement of insurable interest is applied somewhat differently than in property and liability insurance. When the individual taking out the policy is also the insured, there is no legal problem concerning insurable interest. The courts have held that every individual has an unlimited insurable interest in his or her own life and that a person may assign that insurable interest to anyone. In other words, there is no legal limit to the amount of insurance one may take out on one's own life and no legal limitations as to whom one may name as beneficiary.

5 The important question of insurable interest arises when the person taking out the insurance is someone other than the person whose life is concerned. In such cases, the law requires that an insurable interest exists at the time the contract is taken out. There are many relationships that provide the basis for an insurable interest. Husbands and wives have an insurable interest in each other; so do partners. A *corporation may have an insurable interest in the life of one of its *executives. In most cases, a parent has an insurable interest in the life of a child, although the extent of this interest may be limited by *statute. A creditor has an insurable interest in the life of a debtor, although this too is usually confined by statute to the amount of the debt or slightly more.

'Principles and Practice of Insurance', Vaughan, E. J. (John Wiley, 1986)

Text organisation

1. Below are the main ideas of the text, but they are not in the correct order. Put them into the order in which they occur in the text. The first one has been done for you.

	Main idea	Order
(i)	Life insurance indemnity is different from other types of insurance indemnity.	
(ii)	Life insurance is similar to other insurance in regard to insurable risk.	
(iii)	The concept of insurable interest operates differently for life insurance.	
(iv)	Life insurance contingency is different from other types of insurance contingency.	1
(v)	Although death is inevitable, the law of large numbers makes life insurance possible.	
(vi)	An individual has an unlimited insurable interest in his own life.	
(vii)	Only people with an insurable interest in a person can take out life insurance on him/her.	

Comprehension

2. Complete the sentences below with the endings which are correct according to the text. Identify the lines in the text where you find your answer.
   (a) Because life insurance contingency is different from other types of contingency,
      (i) it cannot be insured against.
      (ii) it requires a particular kind of policy.
      (iii) only special insurance companies offer insurance for it.
      (iv) life insurance is very expensive.

   (b) The risk which life insurance insures against is
      (i) whether a person will die.
      (ii) whether a person will die before the age of 50.
      (iii) whether a person dies leaving a dependent family.
      (iv) whether a person dies unexpectedly.

   (c) Indemnity in life insurance is different because
      (i) it is impossible to value a life financially.
      (ii) it is impossible to estimate how much a person will earn in his/her life.
      (iii) a human life has no financial value.
      (iv) the value of a person depends on the age at which he/she dies.

   (d) When a person insures his/her own life,
      (i) only that person can have an insurable interest in himself/herself.
      (ii) any other person can claim an insurable interest in him/her.
      (iii) the law restricts who can be given insurable interest in him/her.
      (iv) he/she can give an insurable interest to any other person.

3. What is the key point when life insurance is bought for one person by another person or organisation? Identify the lines in the text where you find your answer.

4. Look at the list below and decide in which cases an insurable interest can exist, according to the text. Tick (✓) those where there is an insurable interest and put a cross (**x**) where there is not.
   (i) A wife in relation to her husband
   (ii) A business in regard to another company's top manager
   (iii) A person in regard to any of his/her relatives
   (iv) A parent in relation to a son or daughter
   (v) A borrower in relation to a lender
   (vi) A lender in relation to a borrower

Vocabulary

5. Insurance, like other areas of business such as banking and accounting, has its own specialised vocabulary. That is, there are certain words which tend to be used frequently when reading, writing or talking about insurance. The following exercise introduces some more of these words. Also, because this text is taken from an academic book, a number of rather formal words are used instead of more informal

ones. In the exercise below match the specialised and formal words from the text with their more informal equivalents on the right. Try to do this exercise by looking at how these specialised/formal words are used in the text. If possible, don't use a dictionary.

Specialised/formal word	Informal equivalent
(i) contingency (line 3)	(a) final
(ii) eventual (line 6)	(b) fixed
(iii) violate (line 7)	(c) comes up
(iv) untimely (line 8)	(d) early
(v) mechanism (line 13)	(e) not all
(vi) specified (line 14)	(f) possibility
(vii) beneficiary (line 15)	(g) stated
(viii) partial (line 16)	(h) give
(ix) face (line 18)	(i) break
(x) modified (line 21)	(j) person who gains
(xi) assign (line 33)	(k) changed
(xii) arises (line 36)	(l) use

Text 2.2 Health care insurance outstrips inflation

Skim and scan

(a) Read the article quickly and then say what you think is the meaning of 'outstrips' in the title.

(b) Who are (i) BUPA and (ii) Laing and Buisson?

Health care insurance outstrips inflation

1 THE COST of private medical insurance goes up today by an average of about four per cent, nearly three times the rate of inflation.

2 Some elderly subscribers face rises as high as 18 per cent. The rises come at a time when the number of people taking out private medical insurance is falling after several steep above-inflation increases in recent years.

3 This year's increases are the smallest for several years and some subscribers, particularly younger ones, will see no increase at all or even a cut in the cost of premiums.

BUPA, the largest private health group, is increasing premiums by between 10 and 18.2 per cent for older subscribers on higher scales of cover, but some younger people on cheaper policies will get a cut of as much as 15 per cent. Premiums are set to rise again later in the year after the Government's decision in the *Budget to impose a three per cent tax on various forms of insurance, including private medical insurance. A spokesman for BUPA said no decision had yet been taken on how this tax would affect premiums or whether it would be partially absorbed. 4

Although the cost of private medical insurance for individuals is rising, BUPA is freezing the cost of its company scheme until next July and says that from now prices will be reviewed only once a year, instead of twice as in recent years. Mr Roger Hymas, BUPA marketing director, said premiums for elderly people were higher because of the demand they made on medical services. The average cost of a claim made by patients under 60 was £983 last year, but the average cost for those over 60 was £1,390 and premiums reflected the difference.

He said: "We are very conscious that many people have been loyal subscribers without making claims over many years yet find their premiums rise sharply as they get older.

"We are working on a scheme to smooth the cost over a lifetime so that people may pay a little more in their younger years for the sake of minimising increases when they get older."

3 BUPA has also introduced a range of policies which offers lower premiums in return for some restrictions, such as limiting treatment to a local hospital or being treated in an *NHS paybed.

9 Mr Hymas said: "We can often reduce premiums by as much as 15–20 per cent while still retaining the essentials of private cover for people willing to change their type of policy."

10 He said that although increases of four to five per cent were three times the current level of inflation, they represented a major success when the cost of medical care had been rising by 15–20 per cent a year.

11 He said: "We feel the private medical sector has come out of the recession in a remarkably resilient fashion with losses in the number of subscribers of no more than two to three per cent."

12 Laing and Buisson, the health care analyst, said those covered by private medical insurance dropped by more than 280,000 over the past three years.

13 The number covered was 6,339,000 last year compared with the peak of 6,625,000 in 1990. This represents just under 11 per cent of the population and Laing and Buisson estimates the proportion will reach 18 per cent by the year 2000.

'Daily Telegraph' June 1994

Vocabulary

1. Find words in the text which have the same meanings as the definitions listed below. The line numbers show which part of the text you should look at.

Definition	Word(s) in text
Lines 0–26 (i) participants (ii) large (iii) amounts (iv) place Lines 27–50 (v) not passed on (vi) keeping the same (vii) indicated (viii) very quickly (ix) spread more evenly	

Definition	Word(s) in text
Lines 51–87 (x) controls (xi) keeping (xii) positive (xiii) maximum number	

Comprehension

2. The text includes a number of figures. Say what the following figures from the text refer to:
   (i) four per cent
   (ii) 18 per cent (two answers)
   (iii) 10–18.2 per cent
   (iv) 15 per cent
   (v) £983
   (vi) £1,390
   (vii) 15–20 per cent (two answers)
   (viii) 280,000
   (ix) 6,339,000
   (x) 6,625,000

3. The text shows a number of ways in which the situation in relation to private medical insurance is different for younger people compared with older people. Make notes about the differences for the headings listed below.

	Situation for the young	Situation for the old
(i) Price increases		
(ii) Use of medical services		
(iii) Cover provided		
(iv) Average claim made		

4. Decide if the following statements are true or false according to the text. Identify the lines in the text where you find your answers.

Statement	True /false	Line numbers
(i) Price increases this year are as large as for previous years.		
(ii) Government tax policies will affect cost of private medical insurance.		
(iii) The average demand for medical services is the same for young and old.		
(iv) People in future will still have to pay much more for medical insurance as they get older.		
(v) Insurance costs can be cheaper for people willing to accept limited medical care.		
(vi) Medical insurance premiums have risen more than medical treatment costs.		
(vii) The number of people giving up private medical insurance has been relatively small.		

5. (a) What percentage of the British population will be covered by private medical insurance in the year 2000?
   (b) Compared to now, will this figure represent an increase or a decrease in the percentage of the British population with private medical insurance?

Text organisation

6. Conjunctions (words like 'so', 'therefore', 'because') and other linking phrases are very important for showing the logical relationships between ideas in a text. To practise the use of such words, match the conjunctions on the left below with the meanings which they have in the text. Look carefully at how the conjunctions and linkers are used in the text as you choose your answers. The first one is done for you.

Conjunction	Meaning in text
(i) or even (line 14)	however
(ii) but (line 19)	for example
(iii) whether (line 29)	as a result
(iv) because (line 39)	at the same time
(v) yet (line 49)	despite/in spite of the fact that
(vi) so (line 52)	if
(vii) such as (line 58)	nevertheless
(viii) while (line 63)	in order
(ix) although (line 66)	or possibly

Viewpoint

Do you think medical care should be provided privately or by the government? If the government provides it, should it be free for everyone? If not, who should pay?

Unit 3 Pensions and pension funds

In this unit the first text describes how public and private pensions are organised in the United States of America. The second text describes how the contributions of employers and employees towards private pensions are controlled and invested.

Text 3.1 How pensions work in the United States

Pre-reading

In most industrialised countries the government provides at least some pension. Should this cover all a retired person's needs or only be enough to pay for essential needs? What are the advantages and disadvantages of private pensions compared to state pensions?

Skim and scan

(a) How many main types of retirement plan are there now?
(b) What are they called?

How pensions work in the United States

1 A pension is an income payable after a worker retires, usually at the age of 60 or above, depending on the provisions of the particular retirement plan. Pensions can also be paid out earlier if a worker becomes *disabled, or to the survivors of a worker who dies.

2 About 90 percent of all U.S. workers are covered for retirement and disability under *SOCIAL SECURITY. Most of the others are members of some public-employee retirement system. Perhaps half of all workers in the private sector are covered by some form of private pension or *PROFIT-SHARING plan.

3 Modern retirement plans come in two general forms. In a defined-benefit plan the amount of the pension is specified by some formula recognizing the worker's length of service and earning history; then the contributions (from employer and employee) needed to provide the pension are determined. A defined-contribution plan indicates how the contributions are to be determined on behalf of each employee and accumulates these contributions in an interest-earning fund; then, at retirement age, the accumulated fund is applied to provide whatever pension it will.

4 A typical pension plan, of either type, will be a written document of some complexity. Among the detailed provisions that will be found are:

1. The rules that determine which workers are eligible to become plan members;

2. The age or ages at which workers can retire, and any choices they may have with respect to retirement age or to the form of the retirement income;
3. The details of the pension formula (if a defined-benefit plan) or of the contribution formula (if a defined-contribution plan);
4. The rules with respect to the disposition of a worker's pension if he or she leaves employment before retirement age or dies;
5. The arrangements by which the employer and employee contribute to the cost of the benefits provided.

Retirement plans can be classified in terms of the entity that sponsors the plan. When the sponsoring agency is some part of government, the plan is considered to be in the public sector. When the plan is sponsored by an employer, when it arises out of the collective-bargaining process, or when it is arranged on an individual basis by the worker, it is said to be in the private sector.

Private pension plans and state or local government accumulate substantial amounts of money awaiting distribution in the form of pensions. These dollars are invested in virtually every kind of income-producing resource, including *stocks, *bonds, *mortgages, and *real estate. As pension funds have increased, they have become an increasingly important factor in the nation's economy. The actual management of pension-fund assets is often the responsibility of some institutional investor – typically the trust departments of major banks or the investment departments of life insurance companies.

The aging of the American population (there were 25 million people age 65 and over in 1980; an estimated 29.2 million in 1986; and a projected 64.5 million by the year 2030) has given increased economic importance to pension funds. In the United States, public and private funds totaled $1.4 trillion in 1986, representing an enormous force in financial markets. Nevertheless, only slightly more than 40 percent of civilian workers were covered by company-provided pensions in the late 1980s.

'How pensions work in the US', Trowbridge, C.L., in 'Macmillan Family Encyclopaedia' (Macmillan 1988), amended

Text organisation

1. Each of the paragraphs in the text has a particular aim. Match the aims below with the paragraphs which they belong to.

Aim of paragraph	Paragraph number
(i) Make difference between public and private pensions.	
(ii) Define what a pension is.	
(iii) Show future importance of pensions.	
(iv) Show present US pension coverage.	
(v) Describe main features of a pension plan.	
(vi) Show financial structure of pensions.	
(vii) Describe management of a pension fund.	

Comprehension

2 (a) What percentage of American workers are in the social security scheme?
(b) Of those *not* covered by social security, how many are in a public retirement plan?
(c) What proportion of workers in the private sector are included in private pension schemes of some kind?

3 (a) With 'defined-benefit' pension plans, what is decided first: how much a person will receive as a pension or how much he/she must pay to get that amount?
(b) Similarly, for 'defined-contribution' pension plans, what is fixed first: the amount of the pension or how much a person will pay for his/her pension?

4. According to the text, which of the points below are normally stated in a pension plan? Put a tick (✓) if they are included and a cross (**x**) if they are not.
(i) Who will receive the pension if the contributor dies before retirement
(ii) The division of pension costs between employer and employee
(iii) A definition of which workers can receive a pension
(iv) The maximum number of years a person can receive a pension
(v) Discussion of age of retirement and any flexibility allowed about this
(vi) The method by which benefits or contributions are calculated
(vii) The minimum amount an employee must contribute to get a pension
(viii) What will happen to an employee's pension if his/her company goes bankrupt
(ix) How the funds of the particular pension plan will be invested
(x) What will happen to the pension of a person who dies prematurely or stops work early

5. Using the information in paragraph 4, complete the diagram from the following list.
(a) labour and management
(b) government
(c) employee
(d) employer

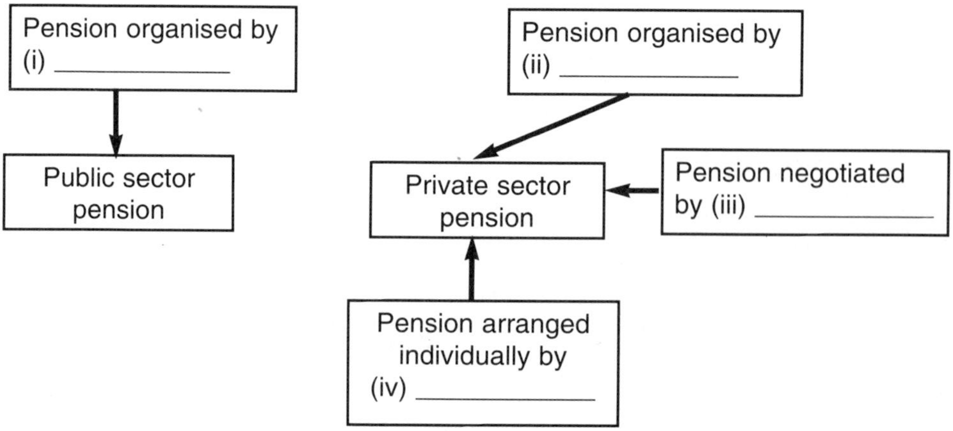

6. Put the following in the order in which they occur in real life, according to the text. Some of the events below are not directly mentioned in the text but can be inferred.

	Event	Order
(i)	Trust departments of banks or insurance investment departments receive pension funds.	
(ii)	Individuals pay pension contributions.	
(iii)	Individuals are paid their pensions when they retire or cannot work any more.	
(iv)	Public and private pension funds gather large amounts of money.	
(v)	Trusts departments and insurance investment departments buy wealth-producing assets.	

7. (a) Is the number of old people in America falling or rising?
   (b) What effect does this rise or fall have on pension funds and, consequently, on the American economy?

Vocabulary

8. (a) Look at how the words and phrases in the box below are used in the text and make sure you understand their meaning.

provisions (line 2)	with respect to (lines 21–22)
defined-benefit plan (line 10)	disposition (line 25)
formula (line 11)	entity (line 29)
defined-contribution plan (line 14)	collective-bargaining process (line 32)
accumulates (line 15)	projected (line 49)
eligible (line 20)	

   (b) Complete the following sentences using the correct word or phrase from the box (in the grammatical form required).
   (i) What regulates the __________ of a pension of an employee who dies before reaching a pensionable age?
   (ii) A __________ states how much an employee will pay each month towards his final pension.
   (iii) According to the __________ of this pension plan, you can receive a pension before 65.
   (iv) __________ our pension scheme, you must work at least ten years to qualify for a pension.
   (v) Under the terms of this __________, you will get a pension of $2,000 a month.
   (vi) The __________ which controls public pensions is the state.
   (vii) The __________ for calculating your annual pension is based on two-thirds monthly salary times number of years of employment.
   (viii) Nobody is __________ to join our company pension scheme until they have been with us for two years.

(ix) The question of pensions for employees is one of the issues which is considered in the __________ .

(x) Because the number of pensioners is __________ to rise in the future, taxes will probably have to be increased.

(xi) As a pension fund receives contributions from individuals, it ____________ large amounts which are placed in various types of investment.

Text 3.2 Control of pension fund investments

Skim and scan

(a) Is the 'Book Reserve Scheme' type of pension more common in Britain or Europe?

(b) Are the majority of pension schemes today 'defined-contribution' or 'defined-benefit' schemes?

Control of pension fund investments

1 It is perfectly possible, although not necessarily wise, for an employer to set up a pension scheme where the benefits are paid out of monies solely provided by the employer out of revenues. Such a scheme would, of course, be heavily dependent upon the consistency of profits of the employer and in most circumstances would not give much security to the pensioner or prospective pensioner. This type of scheme is to be found on the Continent and is generally known as a 'Book Reserve Scheme'.

2 Nearly all employers (and the government by virtue of the *tax exemptions on investment activities which it gives) recognise that a more secure base for the payment of pensions can be achieved by setting aside monies in a *trust fund and investing them in a variety of *Stock Exchange and other *securities. Such a trust fund will consist of the contributions of the employer, the contributions of the employee (in the case of a contributory fund), and the investment income from previously acquired investments and those assets themselves.

3 The management of the trust fund will be carried out by the *trustees who are normally appointed by the employer (but increasingly from names put forward for appointment by an elective process carried out in conjunction with *trade unions and other employee representative bodies).

4 While all the duties of the trustees are extremely important (and they are dealt with elsewhere in this book), among the most onerous is the investment of the trust property.

5 The manner in which the trustees carry out their investment responsibilities will be governed by the trust deed or other instrument under which the pension scheme is constituted. Most, if not all, modern trust deeds will have a specific investment clause which will permit the trustees to invest over a wide range which enables them to take full advantage of the various investment outlets available to them.

6 No matter whether the funds are self-administered, internally or externally managed or wholly managed by an insurance company, the trustees cannot abrogate their responsibility for the investments of the scheme. It is, therefore, important that the essentials of policy-making are fully understood.

7 Investment policy will be a function of the requirements of the scheme. The vast majority of present-day pension schemes are what are known as 'final-salary' or 'defined-benefit' schemes. In this type of scheme, the pension payable is linked to the salary of the pensioner before retirement (perhaps the average of the last five years, three years or, more commonly these days, the salary in the final year).

8 Final-salary schemes have the merit of at least making sure that the pension, when first paid, has taken account of inflationary movements in salaries up to the point of retirement. Such a link is an important factor in the type of investment policy followed.

9 While final-salary schemes are now the most common, the money purchase or defined-contribution schemes cannot be totally ignored (and they have come back into the limelight following the recent decline in the rate of inflation). Clearly, an investment policy designed to cater for inflation, at least to the point of retirement, will be quite different from one which does not attempt to do this.

'Control of pension fund investments' in 'Pension Fund Administration', Shepherd, A.G. (ed.) (ICSA Publishing, 1984), amended.

Vocabulary

1. Look at how the words and phrases in the box are used in the text. Then match them with their definitions below.

exemptions (line 8)	instrument (line 23)
in conjunction with (lines 17–18)	constituted (line 24)
bodies (line 18)	abrogate (line 30)
onerous (line 20)	come back into the limelight (lines 43–44)
governed (line 23)	cater for (line 45)

(i) take into account
(ii) organisations
(iii) document
(iv) demanding
(v) given a structure
(vi) excused payment
(vii) appear again
(viii) controlled
(ix) by agreement with
(x) avoid

Comprehension

2. (a) According to the text, can pensions be paid using only the income which a company earns?

(b) Depending on the answer to 2(a), what does the text say are the advantages or disadvantages of such a system?

3 (a) What are the three sources of income for a pension trust fund?
(b) What encouragement does the government give to pension trust funds, according to the text?

4. Below are some statements regarding the running of pension trust funds. Decide whether they are true or false according to the text.

	Statement	True/false
(i)	Trustees for pension trust funds are the choice only of the employer.	
(ii)	Management of trust property is the only task of pension fund trustees.	
(iii)	There are documents which control how a trust fund can be administered.	
(iv)	Most trusts are forced to invest in a few types of investment.	
(v)	Trustees can hand over decisions about investing to others.	

5. In the following paragraph, choose the alternatives which are correct according to the text.

(Most/Many) pension schemes today are of the ('defined-benefit'/'defined-contribution') type. With this type of scheme the pension depends on the (final salary/average contributions) of the employee. Such pensions (take/do not take) account of increases in inflation. (Defined-benefit schemes/ Defined-contribution schemes), on the other hand, are becoming (less/more) popular now that inflation has (increased/decreased). The investment policies required by both types of pension are (similar/different).

Text organisation

6. Look again at the last paragraph of the text (paragraph 9). When you have read it, look at the three paragraphs in the table on the next page. They continue the text, but they are not in the right order. Arrange them in their correct order by numbering them 10, 11 and 12.

Paragraph	Order
(i) It is against this background that investment policy must be determined. The mix of assets between conventional gilt-edged stocks, index-linked gilt-edged stocks, equities and properties will be a response to the open-ended nature of liabilities in a final-salary scheme.	
(ii) If it is assumed that the type of pension scheme for which investment policy is being determined is of the final-salary type, then certain factors have to be taken into account in its formulation. First, the policy horizon will be a long one. A new entrant to a scheme may have a working life of 30 to 40 years and a further 15 to 20 years on pension.	
(iii) Secondly, there may be certain advantages of such long time horizons: such as the ability to take a view on certain types of initially low-income investments which may have the prospects of growth and capital gain. There are also severe disadvantages in that investment targets for a final-salary type scheme are in many ways open-ended. This is particularly the case where the employer endeavours to take account of inflation by escalating the level of pensions in payment.	

Unit 4 Property insurance

The first text in this unit is from a leaflet offering insurance for a home and its contents. In the second text recent developments in car insurance, such as insuring by telephone, and the resulting increased competition between insurers are looked at.

At Royal Insurance we believe in offering careful householders both buildings and contents insurance at the best possible price. After all if you take steps to protect your home it's only right that we, as one of Britain's leading household insurance companies, should recognise such care by using the fairest, most accurate premium assessment system available today. Your quotation will be tailor made for you – taking into account where you live and the size, type and age of your home.

For many householders the premium could be less than that charged by their present insurer.

HEADING A

At Royal Insurance our professional friendly staff will ensure not only that your claim is dealt with promptly but also without unnecessary argument. After all you want your claim settled without problems and delays.

HEADING B

You can enjoy real peace of mind knowing that your home and its contents are protected by a company who have been providing insurance expertise for over 150 years and whose customer service is second to none – something appreciated by over one million householders who have trusted Royal Insurance to look after their home.

Why should low risk householders *like you* pay high risk premiums

HEADING C

At Royal Insurance we ensure that you know exactly what your insurance covers you for. As for buying a policy from Royal Insurance, nothing could be more

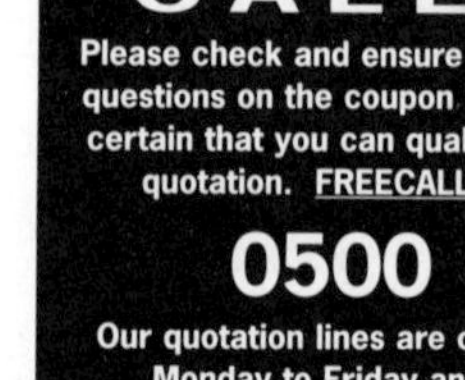

CALL FREE

Please check and ensure that you can tick yes to the six questions on the coupon opposite. If you can, it is almost certain that you can qualify for a lower home insurance quotation. FREECALL now quoting HTGM3524

0500 223344

Our quotation lines are open for calls 8 am – 7.30 pm Monday to Friday and 9 am – 12 pm Saturday.

Text 4.1 Insuring a home and its contents

Pre-reading

How do you think different insurers can offer different quotes to insure the same piece of property? What factors influence how much people have to pay for insurance for their property?

Skim and scan

Below are the headings for the main part of the text. Decide where each belongs and write beside it the correct letter (A–E).

(i) Extra customer care 24 hours a day, 365 days a year
(ii) Easy to understand and simple to buy
(iii) Fast and fair settlement of claims
(iv) Real peace of mind from one of the UK's largest insurance companies
(v) New for old cover

traightforward, you will almost certainly ualify if you can tick 'yes' to the 6 questions pposite. Then complete the coupon and post to us FREEPOST (you don't need a stamp) or all us on FREECALL 0500 223344 and we will end you a free quotation by return of post.

Many insurance companies will only pay you he original cost of the items for which you make a claim. With Royal Insurance, however, ou enjoy extra peace of nind with 'new for old over'. This means that ve'll replace items laimed for at today's prices, if they cannot be conomically repaired. No reductions will be nade for wear and tear, except for clothing, ousehold linen and pedal cycles.

HEADING E

FREE 24 hour helpline and emergency repair service. Should you unfortunately suffer an emergency like a burst pipe or tiles blown off your roof, simply call our FREEPHONE 24 hour emergency number, any day of the year. We will provide practical help from a competent local tradesman and we will pick up the bill up to £150 for each call out necessary.

VALUABLE DISCOUNTS OFF CONTENTS PREMIUMS SEE OVERLEAF FOR DETAILS

FOLD

NO OBLIGATION

YOU MAY QUALIFY FOR A LOWER HOME INSURANCE QUOTATION IF YOU CAN TICK YES TO THE 6 POINTS BELOW.

1. My home has no more than five bedrooms. ❑
2. My home is built of brick or stone, with a slate or tiled roof. ❑
3. This property is my main dwelling. ❑
4. I have had no more than one claim in the last three years and this did not amount to more than £1,000. ❑
5. I do not use my home for business (other than clerical use). ❑
6. My home was built after 1871. ❑

NOW PLEASE ANSWER THE 4 QUESTIONS BELOW

Is your home? a House ❑ a Bungalow ❑ or Flat ❑ (with its own separate lockable entrance under your sole control).

Is it? Detached ❑ Semi-detached ❑ Terraced ❑

How many bedrooms is it designed to have? ❑

When was it built? 1871–1919 ❑ 1920–45 ❑ 1946–79 ❑ or 1980 on ❑

PLEASE TELL US A LITTLE ABOUT YOURSELF.

Mr/Mrs/Miss/Ms
Surname ....
Forenames ....
Are you? .... Single ❑ Married ❑ Widowed ❑ or Divorced ❑
Address ....
.... Postcode ....
Occupation ....
Date of Birth ..... / ..... / .... Spouse's Date of Birth ..... / ..... / ....
Telephone Numbers (please include S.T.D. code)
Daytime .... Evening ....
When does your present policy expire? ..... / ..... / ....
Present insurer ....
In certain locations security may be a prerequisite. HTGM3524

PLUS See if you can qualify for any of this range of valuable contents premium discounts. Please tick any or all of the relevant boxes.

15% OCCUPANCY DISCOUNT
My home is normally occupied during the day ❑
5% PHYSICAL SECURITY DISCOUNT I have 5 lever mortice locks on all external doors and key operated window locks ❑
10% NEIGHBOURHOOD/HOME WATCH DISCOUNT I live in a neighbourhood/ homewatch area ❑
10% BURGLAR ALARM DISCOUNT I have a professionally installed burglar alarm with an annual maintenance contract ❑
15% OVER 50 DISCOUNT You will automatically save 15% on your contents and buildings premiums if you or your spouse are aged 50 or over.

This offer is not available in Northern Ireland or Republic of Ireland

MOISTEN HERE

MOISTEN HERE

Text organisation

1. What do the following pronouns in the text refer to? (If you are not using the book in sequence, see Unit 1, Text 2, question 1 before you begin this exercise.)

Pronoun	Refers to	Line number
(i) we (line 1)		
(ii) it (line 6)		
(iii) you (line 11)		
(iv) their (line 15)		
(v) its (line 27)		
(vi) their (line 34)		
(vii) it (line 44)		
(viii) us (lines 44, 45)		
(ix) This (line 53)		
(x) they (line 55)		

Comprehension

2. (a) In paragraph 1 what kind of householders do Royal Insurance hope to attract?
   (b) If one of these householders applies for insurance, how do Royal Insurance decide what the premium of that household should be?
   (c) What could be the benefit of such a premium quotation for a householder?

3. What two things do Royal Insurance promise will happen if a householder makes an insurance claim?

4. (a) How long have Royal Insurance been in business?
   (b) How many homes are presently insured by Royal Insurance?

5. Using the information in paragraphs 5 and 6, complete the sentences below so that they are true according to the text.
   (i) __________ if you take out a policy with Royal Insurance.
   (ii) You will be eligible to take out a household insurance policy with Royal Insurance if__________
   (iii) If you return the coupon or phone them, __________
   (iv) Royal Insurance __________ when you make a claim for lost or damaged articles.
   (v) Other insurance companies __________ when you make a claim for lost or damaged articles.

6. Which of the following services do Royal Insurance provide if you take out a household insurance policy with them? Write 'yes' or 'no' and identify the lines in the text where you find your answers.

Service	Provided by Royal (yes/no)	Line numbers
(i) Sending their own employees to deal with emergency house repairs		
(ii) Help and information in dealing with emergency house repairs any time		
(iii) Unlimited payment to cover the cost of any emergency house repairs		
(iv) Arranging for someone in the policy holder's area to deal with an emergency repair.		

7. Looking at the application form for obtaining household insurance from Royal Insurance, decide which of the following applications might qualify for a lower home insurance quotation. If they do not qualify, say why.
   (a) A hairdresser working at home has a 1931 four-bedroom house built of brick with a tiled roof. He owns no other property and has never claimed on a household insurance policy.
   (b) A marketing manager for a big company has just bought a newly-built house. It is constructed from local stone and has a slate roof. It is a large five-bedroom house. She also owns a holiday cottage on the coast but only uses it for a few weeks in the year. Last year there was a robbery at her holiday cottage and she claimed £750 from her insurance company.
   (c) A pensioner lives in a one-bedroom terrace house built in the mid-nineteenth century. All the houses in her street are red-brick with tiled roofs. The last claim this person made on her household insurance policy was in 1975 when there were floods. On that occasion she claimed £1,500 for necessary household repairs. She was left another house by her parents but sold it many years ago.

Vocabulary

8. Because this leaflet was designed to appeal personally to people, it is written in an informal style. Look at how the words and expressions on the left are used in the text. Then match them with their more formal equivalent on the right.

Informal word/expression	Formal equivalent
(i) contents (line 3)	(a) especially designed
(ii) take steps (line 5)	(b) settle an account
(iii) tailor made (line 11)	(c) household possessions
(iv) taking into account (lines 11–12)	(d) serenity
(v) peace of mind (line 26)	(e) receive full compensation
(vi) second to none (lines 30–31)	(f) bear in mind
(vii) 'new for old cover' (lines 52–53)	(g) damage through use
(viii) wear and tear (line 57)	(h) do what is required
(ix) pick up the bill (lines 68–69)	(i) cannot be bettered

9. Look at the application form and find words and expressions which have the meanings given below.
   (i) have the right to join
   (ii) a one-storey house standing alone
   (iii) a house joined to onc other house
   (iv) a house attached to many other houses
   (v) a man or woman whose wife or husband has died
   (vi) husband or wife
   (vii) finish
   (viii) an essential requirement
   (ix) being lived in
   (x) special type of security for doors
   (xi) local organisation to improve security

Text 4.2 Shop around for the best car insurance

Skim and scan

(a) What is the meaning of 'Shop around' in the headline of this article?
(b) Who are 'Telesure', 'Direct Line' and 'Guardian Direct'?

Shop around for the best car insurance

1 Shopping around for motor insurance really pays. You might find a quote for half your present premium if you just took time to make a few telephone calls.

2 Research by Telesure, one of the new telephone-based insurance brokers, found differences in premiums of more than 100 per cent in some cases, and 30 or 40 per cent in many. That can easily mean a saving of £100 or more. "I think that rating, overall, is very random," says Simon Ward, Telesure's chief executive.

3 Insurers set their rates in line with their own claims' experience. So, if your insurer has had a lot of these from drivers with your model of car, or living in your area, your premiums could rise. Another insurer with far fewer claims would offer you a much better rate.

4 But if your renewal is due next month, and you start to shop around now, you cannot rely on getting the same rate in a few weeks. Premiums can change significantly from month to month, let alone year to year or between companies.

5 There are many loyal (or lazy) customers who renew every year with the same company assuming that, if their premiums are rising, other companies will be raising rates in the same way.

6 Unfortunately that is not necessarily the case: your insurer will have no compunction about bumping up rates for existing customers, while a rival might be keen to attract new business and would make you a much better offer. Most insurers will accept

transferred *no-claims bonuses, so you do not have to feel tied.

The motor insurance market is just emerging from a period of steep price rises – more than 20 per cent a year – to compensate for horrendous claim rates due to crime and the recession. The industry is also changing shape as the arrival of Direct Line, the cost-cutting, telephone-based direct insurer, and its imitators force the old giants of the insurance world to re-think their strategies.

Some sections of the motor insurance industry are now murmuring about a price war. That could be exaggerated, but companies moving into the direct insurance market need to grab a big-enough share of the market to justify the huge investment in computer systems, staff training and so on.

The easiest way to build up market share is to offer low premiums, even if that means making a loss for the first few years. And if *direct writers are lowering premiums, the rest of the industry will fight back.

So, consumers could benefit, at least in the short term. Indeed, things are looking better for car owners than they have for some time.

If insurers want to avoid a price war, 11
they may start trying to compete on other factors, such as service – promising to offer smoother claims procedures, for example. This appears to be the direction being taken by the latest entrant to the direct market, Guardian Direct.

It is, however, far less easy for 12
consumers to shop around for good service than for low prices. The proof of good service really comes when you claim – which, with any luck, will be long after you have made your choice.

There can be some confusion between 13
direct insurers and telephone brokers, especially as both tend to advertise widely with cheap insurance offers.

Direct insurers are those which sell 14
only their own policies, and only directly to the consumer over the telephone. They cut out third parties, which reduces administrative costs, and should allow them to charge less.

Telephone brokers have access to 15
quotes from many different insurers, and use a computer to find the lowest for you. Some of them deal with a select panel of a dozen insurers, while others quote for more than 100.

'The Financial Times' March 5–6 1994

Text organisation

1. We have looked earlier at the important role of pronouns in texts. The two exercises below give further practice in understanding the use of pronouns. (If you are not using this book in sequence, see Unit 1, Text 2, question 1 before you begin the exercises.)
   (a) What do the following pronouns refer to in the text? Give line references for your answers.

Pronoun	Refers to	Line numbers
(i) That (line 9) (ii) their (line 14) (iii) these (line 16) (iv) their (line 31) (v) that (line 34) (vi) its (line 40) (vii) That (line 46) (viii) they (line 60) (ix) This (line 66) (x) It (line 69)		

(b) Find the pronoun(s) which refer(s) to these items in the text.
   (i) 'Insurers' (line 62)
   (ii) 'direct insurers' (line 76) and 'telephone brokers' (line 76)
   (iii) 'Direct insurers' (line 79)
   (iv) Telephone brokers (line 85)

Comprehension

2. Decide if the following statements are true or false according to the text. Identify the line(s) where you find your answer in each case.

	Statement	True/false	Line numbers
(i)	You can always save 50% on your car insurance if you phone around.		
(ii)	Differences in car insurance premiums between companies can be up to double.		
(iii)	A difference between car insurance premiums of at least 30% can always be found when you look around.		

3. Tick (✓) the factors below, which affect how much insurance premium a person must pay, according to the text. Put a cross (**x**) if the factor is not mentioned in the text or does not affect the premium.
   (i) How long a company has been providing car insurance
   (ii) How many accidents your type of car has had with a particular insurance company
   (iii) How long before renewal you ask for a premium quote
   (iv) The length of time you have been with an insurance company
   (v) Asking for a car insurance quote from a company which is not your present insurer

4. (a) What does the figure 20 per cent (line 35) represent?
   (b) What was the cause of this figure of 20 per cent?
   (c) Why do you think the recession has had an effect on this figure?

5. Complete the following sentences so that they are correct according to the text.
   (a) The established insurance companies are changing because
      (i) they want to prevent direct insurers entering the market.
      (ii) they don't feel the direct insurers are a threat.
      (iii) they fear the competition of the new direct insurers.
      (iv) they have taken over the new direct insurers.
   (b) Direct insurers have a very aggressive pricing policy because
      (i) their overheads are low.
      (ii) they need to cover high capital costs.
      (iii) they have a lot of finance capital behind them.
      (iv) they want to drive the established insurance companies out of the market.
   (c) Direct insurers will offer low prices even if
      (i) they lose money at the beginning.
      (ii) the established companies do the same.
      (iii) this doesn't rapidly increase sales of their policies.
      (iv) this damages the whole insurance industry.

6. (a) If insurers don't compete on price, in what other way could they compete?
   (b) What example does the text give of this other way of competing?
   (c) What does the writer of this text think of this other form of competition, as compared to price competition?

7. For the list of points below, write 'DI' for those which, according to the text, are true about direct insurance, and 'TB' for those which are true about telephone brokers.
   (i) Use hi-tech equipment to locate the lowest possible insurance premium for a customer.
   (ii) Only sell insurance policies written by themselves.
   (iii) Deal directly with the person wanting insurance.
   (iv) Get quotes from over 100 different insurers.
   (v) Sell insurance from a limited number of insurance companies.
   (vi) Only use the telephone to sell to potential customers.
   (vii) Do not use the telephone to get insurance quotes.

Vocabulary

8. Find words in the text which have the same meanings as the definitions listed on the next page. The line numbers show which part of the text you should look at.

Definition	Word(s) in text
Lines 1–20 (i) dependent on chance (ii) type Lines 21–32 (iii) insure something again (iv) not to mention (v) guilt (vi) increasing (vii) to consider yourself unable to escape Lines 33–68 (viii) people who do the same thing (ix) talking quietly (x) person or company joining something	

Viewpoint

Some people are finding it increasingly difficult to get insurance of various kinds for themselves, for example, elderly people wanting health insurance or people living in areas with a lot of crime who want car insurance. Insurance companies say they refuse to insure such people in order to keep premiums down for the majority of people. Do you think insurance companies are correct to follow such a policy? Is there another way of dealing with high-risk people who want insurance?

Unit 5 Credit insurance

In this unit the first text looks at the various kinds of credit insurance (e.g. against a company not paying for exports it has been sent) which are available to companies. The second text examines how changes to the export credit insurance system in Germany will have important effects on companies in that country.

Text 5.1 Different types of credit cover

Pre-reading

What kind of risks do companies face in doing business? What additional risks are there for companies which export or import goods compared to those companies which only do business in their own country? Against which of these various risks do you think credit insurance can protect a business?

Skim and scan

(a) What do you think is the meaning of 'cover' as used in the title and text?
(b) To which areas of the world does 'multi-market insurance' apply?

Different types of credit cover

• HEADING A

1 Offered by a number of underwriters in the UK and on the continent, this policy structure protects against the catastrophe risk. Sometimes called "Excess of Loss" or "Stop Loss cover", the underwriting philosophy is centred around the insured's existing in-house credit management controls.

2 The insured will agree a "first loss" or non-qualifying loss designed to eliminate predictable lower level losses.

3 Bad debt losses in excess of this level accumulate within a second pre-determined band or layer, referred to as the annual aggregate.

4 A layer of cover is then purchased in excess of this self-insured proportion.

5 Cover of up to 100% of each qualifying loss in excess of this agreed annual aggregate is available.

6 The cover is normally fixed up to an agreed ceiling of annual losses, known as the "maximum liability".

• HEADING B

7 This is the more traditional credit insurance policy, normally protecting all sales under a single policy. The policy provides the credit manager with up-to-date

financial advice on all principal customers. Generally the insured will self-insure an element of each credit limit. Normally indemnity is 80% – 85%.

8 At commencement of the policy an assessment is made of turnover likely to be declared under the policy.

9 The underwriter will agree an annual premium rate charged against such declarations, usually quarterly.

• HEADING C

10 Some insurers now offer pre-delivery cover as an additional element of whole turnover cover. Indemnity is the same as normal credit risk and premium is either charged as an additional rate on turnover or is combined in a single charge.

• HEADING D

11 More companies are now expanding their export business and require a simple, cost effective credit insurance policy which does not automatically provide unnecessary political risk cover. Multi market insurance has been designed to provide cover in a single policy against the risk of non-payment, due to insolvency or protracted default, in the UK and most *OECD markets.

12 All credit risks are covered with 90% indemnity for both UK and export sales. Financial advice is also available on major buyers.

• HEADING E

13 Occasionally one debtor may represent an inordinately large element of a company's turnover. Although one argument suggests that if the buyer is undoubted, then credit insurance cover is not necessary, the catastrophic effect of non-payment, due to unforeseeable or uncontrollable events, would invariably suggest otherwise.

14 Principal customer cover provides protection against non-payment through insolvency of larger buyers. The benefit of financial advice is available and indemnities vary between 70% – 90%.

15 This type of cover is sometimes referred to as "Datum Line" cover.

• HEADING F

16 Insures individual target risks or the large single contract. Premium can be charged as a percentage rate on insured sales, but is more likely to be calculated as a rate on contract value. Indemnity varies from 75% to 100%, dependent upon the quality of risk.

• HEADING G

17 Insures the advance payments made to a supplier prior to receipt of goods. The policy can also be extended to cover consequential loss which may be incurred if the supplier defaults. Policies are usually underwritten on a single contract basis with premium charged as a fixed amount on contract value. Indemnity up to 100% is available.

'A Credit to the Company', Credit Insurance Association Ltd (1993)

Text organisation

1. Below is a list of the headings in the text. Identify them as Headings A–G. You do not need to understand all the vocabulary of the headings to do this exercise.
   (i) Pre-delivery Risk cover
   (ii) Supplier Default – Consequential Loss cover
   (iii) Principal Customer cover
   (iv) Catastrophe cover
   (v) Multi-market policy
   (vi) Whole Turnover cover
   (vii) Specific Account – Single Contract cover

Vocabulary

2. Some of the words in this text are quite difficult because they are formal or used with a specialised meaning. Look at how the words on the left are used in the text and then match them to the more informal equivalents on the right.

Formal specialised word	Informal equivalent
(i) underwriters (line 1)	get rid of
(ii) eliminate (line 5)	expected
(iii) accumulate (line 7)	thought sure to pay
(iv) pre-determined (lines 7–8)	occur
(v) declared (line 19)	before
(vi) insolvency (line 30)	always
(vii) protracted (line 30)	risk analysts
(viii) default (line 30)	decided beforehand
(ix) inordinately (line 33)	failure to pay
(x) undoubted (line 35)	resulting
(xi) invariably (line 37)	having gone out of business
(xii) prior to (line 46)	extremely
(xiii) consequential (line 47)	lasting a long time
(xiv) be incurred (lines 47–48)	are added together

Comprehension

3. On the left below are a list of some types of credit insurance available to businesses. On the right are figures showing how much of the risk is insured (i.e. has indemnity). Match each figure to the correct type of credit insurance according to the text.

Type of credit insurance	Amount of risk covered
(i) Specific Account	100% (above agreed amount of loss)
(ii) Supplier Default	90%
(iii) Whole Turnover	75–100%
(iv) Catastrophe	up to 100%
(v) Multi-market	70–90%
(vi) Principal Customer	80–85%

4. (a) The diagram below illustrates the structure of 'Catastrophe cover' as described in lines 1–15. Using that information, complete the diagram with the following.
   (i) annual aggregate
   (ii) maximum liability
   (iii) 100% cover
   (iv) 'first loss'

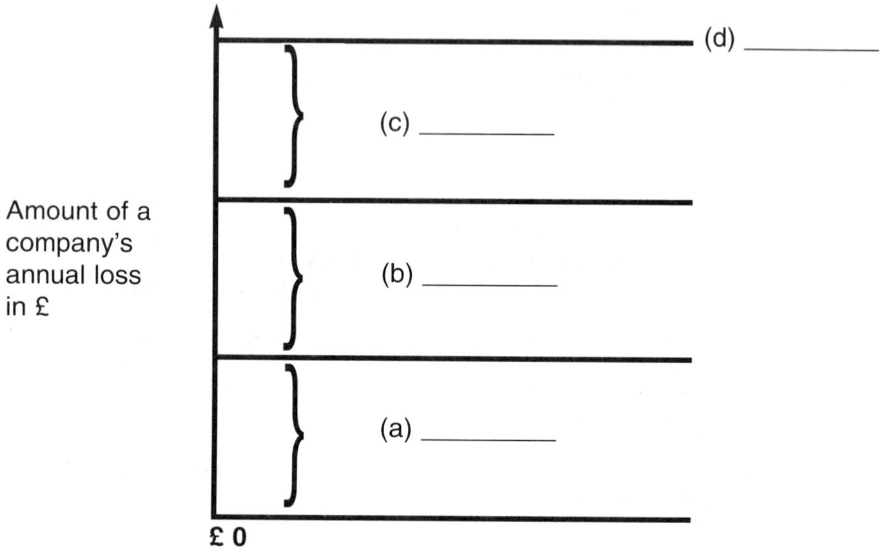

(b) For each of the following in regard to 'Catastrophe cover', say who pays for any loss: the company seeking insurance or the insurance company. Identify the lines in the text where you find your answers.
   (i) first loss
   (ii) annual aggregate
   (iii) amount above annual aggregate up to an agreed annual limit

5. Below is a chart representing three types of credit insurance policies. On the next page there are various statements. Match each statement to the type of policy it refers to, according to the text, by putting the letter in the correct box.

Whole Turnover	Pre-delivery Risk	Multi-market

(a) This policy does not always insure against political events.
(b) This policy has probably been the most used one for credit insurance up to now.
(c) 15–20 per cent of the credit limit is not covered by this policy.
(d) This policy is usually taken out together with whole turnover cover.
(e) This policy covers the seller against non-payment by a buyer in Britain and most OECD countries.
(f) Policies of this kind provide information about the financial situation of large customers a company is considering selling to.
(g) This policy does not cover the first 10 per cent of any loss.
(h) The cost of this policy is normally paid four times a year and is based on the estimated annual amount of a company's sales.
(i) The cost of this policy is either added to or included in the cost of a whole turnover policy.

6. Complete the sentence below with ending (i), (ii), (iii) or (iv) so that it is correct according to the text. Note the lines in the text where you find your answer.

If one customer buys a very large percentage of a company's sales,
(i) insurance against that buyer failing to pay cannot be obtained.
(ii) there is no argument in favour of not needing insurance against that buyer failing to pay.
(iii) it is clear that insurance against that buyer failing to pay is necessary.
(iv) it is inevitable that at some stage that buyer will fail to pay.

7. (a) What is the other name for 'Principal Customer cover'?
(b) List the three main features of Principal Customer cover as mentioned in the text.

8. Below are some statements about 'Specific Account – Single Contract cover' and 'Supplier Default – Consequential Loss cover'. Say whether the statements are true or false according to the text.

	Specific Account – Single Contract cover/ Supplier Default – Consequential Loss cover	True/false
(i)	The degree of risk involved in a sale determines how much insurance can be obtained.	
(ii)	This type of cover only be used to insure a single sale.	
(iii)	The premium is only calculated in one way.	
(iv)	It is not possible to insure against total loss.	
(v)	This insurance covers losses both before and after a buyer receives goods ordered.	
(vi)	The premium of this insurance is fixed in relation to each contract.	

Text 5.2 Five-tier rate system controversial

Skim and scan

(a) Explain the meaning of 'Five-tier rate system' in the title of this text.
(b) What is 'Hermes'?

Five-tier rate system controversial

1 Germany's export credit insurance system came of age on July 1 with the abandonment of a 50-year-old system of uniform premium rates. A five-tier system was introduced which effectively reduced the former standard premium by two-thirds for cover on deals with lowest-risk countries, and doubled it for companies doing business with the world's economic laggards.

2 While the government saw the change as an occasion for celebration, industry and the opposition remained as resolutely glum as they had through more than two years of consultation.

3 Certain media commentators were downright aggressive. One leading newspaper, for example, described the move as an insurance policy for the Bonn government paid for by exporters. East German politicians complained that because of the heavier premiums for deals with their manufacturers' traditional Russian and other east bloc countries, export credit insurance would now exclusively benefit west German companies.

4 Bonn was insistent that the changes should go through. Germany was behind the times, it said, being the only major exporter to apply uniform tariffs. It also had international agreements to honour: subsidy rules in the *General Agreement on Tariffs and Trade required export credit insurance schemes to be independent and self-supporting. The old system was increasingly failing to meet these criteria.

5 At the same time, the Bonn administration was under strict orders from the Bundesbank to cut state spending wherever possible. Mounting deficits in the state-sponsored Hermes insurance programme, administered by the Allianz group, were a clear target. The federal budget subsidised the Hermes programme to the tune of a record DM5.1bn last year, and a further escalation to DM7.5bn (regardless of the impact of the new premiums) has already been earmarked for the current year.

As Günter Rexrodt, economics minister, pointed out recently, DM4.5bn of the 1993 Hermes deficit was due to outstanding debts from the former Soviet Union. While he failed to mention that countries such as Russia and the Ukraine – still important outlets for east Germany's struggling industry – had been placed in the worst risk grade, he made much of cheaper premiums for other countries where west German exporters are hoping to find new growth.

Singapore, Taiwan and South Korea are now in the top rank – "countries without special risks". For export credit insurance purposes, they are now on equal terms with large industrialised nations for which the services of Hermes play no role. Premiums on deals with China and the Czech Republic are reduced by a third.

Mr Rexrodt insisted that higher premiums for Russia and former Soviet Union states offered no disadvantages to German exporters, since competing nations had long since been paying more for cover there.

While the minister side-stepped the implications for east Germany, his ministry officials had earlier ridden rough-shod over protests. At a March meeting in the Baltic state of Mecklenburg-Vorpommern, regional leaders protested that Hermes operated exclusively on behalf of west German interests. A Hermes representative was able to demonstrate the charge as untrue with figures which at the same time starkly illustrated just how important the system was to the region's economy. While Hermes covered 6 per cent at most of all German exports, the proportion rose to 50 per cent in the former *GDR.

'Financial Times' 7 July 1994

Text organisation

1. Below are the main ideas of the nine paragraphs of the text. Write down the number of the paragraph that each one belongs to.

	Main idea of paragraph	Paragraph number
(i)	Eastern Germany's main ex-communist trading partners rated most risky to trade with in the new system.	
(ii)	Some people think the new system chiefly benefits western German companies.	
(iii)	The government rejected complaints that the export insurance system only helps western German companies.	
(iv)	Industry in Germany was less happy about the new system than the government.	
(v)	Under the new system, export insurance now costs less to strong Asian economies.	
(vi)	The system of one export insurance premium was replaced by a variable premium system.	
(vii)	The German government wanted to cut its large expenditure on the export insurance program.	
(viii)	The former German insurance system had to change to meet international requirements.	
(ix)	All countries had higher export insurance charges for ex-communist states, not only Germany.	

Comprehension

2. (a) How long had Germany had its previous export credit insurance system?
   (b) From the percentages in the box, choose the ones which fit the two descriptions below, referring to the new German export insurance system.

200%	33%	100%	75%	66%

   (i) The amount by which the insurance premium for low-risk countries has been reduced
   (ii) The amount by which the insurance premium for high-risk countries has been increased

3. (a) Why is the new export insurance system criticised in former East Germany?
   (b) How do businesses in western Germany seem to benefit from the new insurance system? (The answer to this question is implied rather than directly stated in the text.)
   (c) What main advantage does the German government hope to get from the new insurance scheme?

4. (a) What does the General Agreement on Tariffs and Trade demand of export credit insurance schemes?
   (b) Was the previous German export insurance scheme meeting this requirement?

5. Show the correct amounts for the following items which relate to the Hermes export insurance programme.

Item	Amount in Deutschmarks
(i) The amount of Hermes' expenditure which related to Russia in 1993	
(ii) The amount which the German government gave Hermes in 1993	
(iii) The amount which Hermes was likely to cost in 1994	

6. Match the countries or regions on the left with the statements on the right about the new premiums which are paid for insurance by German companies when they export to them. Some statements apply to more than one country or region.

Country or region	Situation regarding premiums
(i) Russia and the Ukraine	(a) Hermes does not insure exports to it/them.
(ii) Russia and former USSR states	(b) Export insurance is two-thirds what it was.
(iii) Singapore, Taiwan, South Korea	(c) Insurance cost is now similar to what other countries pay.
(iv) China	(d) Premiums are now twice as high.
(v) Czech Republic	(e) Regarded as the same as an advanced country.
(vi) Major industrial countries	(f) Cost most to insure exports.

7. Say whether the following statements are true or false. Identify the lines in the text where you find your answers.
   (i) Mr Rexrodt stated clearly the effect the new export insurance system would have for eastern Germany.
   (ii) Mr Rexrodt's officials have rejected criticism of the new export insurance system.
   (iii) There have been regional protests in Germany that the system only benefits western Germany.
   (iv) Figures regarding the Hermes insurance system support protests of the regional leaders about it.
   (v) The Hermes system insures a much higher percentage of exports from western Germany than from eastern Germany.

Vocabulary

8. This text was taken from a newspaper and often such articles use a mixture of formal and informal vocabulary. Look at how the words and expressions on the left below are used in the text and then mark them 'F' if you think they are formal and 'I' if you think they are informal. Then match each one to its formal or informal equivalent on the right. The first one is done for you.

	Word/ expression in text	Formal/ informal	Formal/informal equivalent
(i)	came of age (line 2) →	I → reached maturity	unhappy
(ii)	laggards (9)		avoided
(iii)	glum (12)		reached maturity
(iv)	insistent (24)		for a sum equal to
(v)	to the tune of (41)		considered most creditworthy
(vi)	escalation (42)		totally disregarded
(vii)	earmarked (44)		are not utilised
(viii)	outstanding (48)		uncompromising
(ix)	in the top rank (57)		clearly
(x)	play no role (61)		quick rise
(xi)	side-stepped (69)		slow payers
(xii)	ridden rough-shod over (71)		unpaid
(xiii)	on behalf of (75)		set aside
(xiv)	starkly (78)		in support of

Text organisation

9. Below are the four sentences which make up the next paragraph of the text you have read. Put these sentences in their correct order. Before you do this, read the last paragraph of the main text again, as this will help you with the exercise.

	Sentence	Order
(i)	Any companies still concentrating on the former Soviet Union should re-examine their strategies.	
(ii)	Small and medium-sized companies especially should not place their faith in the eastern market, he said.	
(iii)	But Hans Birner from the federal economics ministry could offer nothing more than a repeat of Bonn's earlier urgings that east German industry should find new markets.	
(iv)	Their chances lay in the west.	

Unit 6 Insurance policies

In this unit we are going to look at the language used in insurance policies. Different parts of one insurance policy will be studied to see the rather special way in which insurance policies are expressed.

Text 6.1 Property insurance

Pre-reading

What elements do you think are included in most insurance policies? What do you think the language used in insurance policies is like? How is it different from everyday spoken and written language?

Skim and scan

(a) Does this section of the insurance policy deal with car insurance, building and contents insurance or health insurance?

(b) Two of the four headings below belong in the text at points A and B. Decide which of the headings belongs at A and which at B.

(i) Inflation protection
(ii) Additional cover
(iii) Your liability as property owner
(iv) Loss or damage

Check your skim and scan answers immediately.

Property insurance

SECTION 1

A

We will pay for loss of or damage to the buildings caused by

1 Fire, Lightning, Explosion or Earthquake

2 Smoke

but not loss or damage caused by smog, agricultural or industrial operations or any gradual process

3 Riot, Civil Commotion, Labour or Political Disturbance

4 Collision with the buildings directly caused by any moving object originating outside your home

but not loss of or damage to hedges, gates or fences by falling trees or branches

5 Storm or Flood
but not
a) loss of or damage to hedges, gates or fences
b) loss or damage caused by frost

6 Theft or Attempted Theft
but not
a) loss or damage by any paying guest or tenant
b) after your home has been unoccupied for more than 30 consecutive days

7 Vandalism or Malicious Acts
but not
a) loss or damage by any paying guest or tenant
b) after your home has been unoccupied for more than 30 consecutive days

8 Escape of Water or Oil from any fixed water or heating installation or from any domestic appliance
but not after your home has been unoccupied for more than 30 consecutive days

9 Subsidence or Heave of the site on which the building of your home stands or Landslip
but not
a) loss or damage caused by
i) coastal or river erosion
ii) demolition, structural repairs or alterations to the buildings
iii) defective design, faulty workmanship or the use of defective materials in the buildings
b) loss of or damage to solid floor slabs resulting from their movement unless the foundations beneath the external walls of your home are damaged at the same time by the same cause
c) loss of or damage to outdoor swimming pools, tennis courts, patios, terraces, service tanks, drains, septic tanks, pipes and cables, central heating fuel storage tanks, drives, footpaths, garden walls, hedges, gates or fences unless your home, an outbuilding or garage is damaged at the same time by the same cause
d) the amount of the "Subsidence" excess shown in the schedule which will apply to any claim for subsidence or heave or landslip

B

1 Plumbing installation

We will pay for damage to any part of the plumbing installation in your home caused by freezing or bursting
but not
a) if the installation is outside or in an outbuilding
b) loss or damage due to rust, corrosion or wear and tear
c) after your home has been unoccupied for more than 30 consecutive days

2 Service Pipes and Cables

We will pay for accidental damage for which you are legally responsible to underground drains, pipes, cables and tanks providing services to or from your home

3 Glass and Sanitary Wear

We will pay for accidental breakage of fixed glass in windows, in doors or in roofs, fixed ceramic hobs or fixed sanitary ware in your home

but not

a) breakage by any paying guest or tenant
b) after your home has been unoccupied for more than 30 consecutive days

4 Fees and Clearance Costs

We will pay

a) the cost of architects, surveyors, consultants and legal fees

but not fees for preparing any claim under this policy

b) costs to clear the site and make it and the buildings safe

necessarily incurred with our consent in the repair or reinstatement of the buildings following damage recoverable under this section

5 *Local Authority Requirements

We will pay the extra cost of reinstatement or repair of the damaged part of the buildings incurred solely to comply with any government or local authority requirement following damage recoverable under this section

but not if such requirement had been advised to you before the damage occurred

6 Alternative Accommodation and Rent

We will pay in addition to any other amount recoverable under this section

a) if you occupy your home
the cost of reasonable alternative accommodation for you, your family and domestic pets
b) if your home is lent or let
rent you would have received but lose

while your home is unfit to live in following damage recoverable under this section
Any claim payment will not be more than 20% of the sum insured by this section

7 Sale and Purchase

a) if you are selling your home the purchaser will have the benefit of the insurance by this section up to the date of completion provided the buildings are not otherwise insured
b) if you are purchasing another private dwelling your new dwelling will be insured by this section for up to three months from the date contracts to purchase are exchanged or in Scotland the date of the acceptance of offer
but not
i) if it is otherwise insured
ii) after completion of the purchase
iii) for more than 125% of the sum insured by this section.

Specimen Home Insurance Policy, Direct Line Insurance

Text organisation

1. In a document such as this, which has legal status, there must be no doubt what is meant. Therefore it is very important that the logical structure is clear. What pronouns and other words and phrases are referring to must be understood. To see how these connections work, write down what the following words in the text refer to. The first one has been done for you.

Word(s)	Refer(s) to
(i) We (line 1)	the company offering this insurance policy (not directly mentioned in the text, but clear from the context)
(ii) the buildings (line 1)	
(iii) their (line 35)	
(iv) your (line 36)	
(v) the same time (line 42)	
(vi) the same cause (line 42)	
(vii) the site (line 66)	
(viii) this section (line 68)	
(ix) such requirement (line 73)	
(x) it (line 94)	

Comprehension

2. Look at the paragraph headings in Part A of the text. In the chart below, tick (✓) those causes of loss or damage which are covered by this policy and identify the paragraphs that give you your answers. Put a cross (**x**) next to any cause of loss or damage which is not insured.

Possible cause of loss or damage	Covered by this policy?	Paragraph number
(i) There is movement of the land under your house.		
(ii) Political protestors are chased on to your property by police.		
(iii) A bomb is dropped during a war between your country and another.		
(iv) Your house is confiscated by the government of your country.		

3. In Part A, certain causes of damage are not covered by this insurance policy. For each of the sentences below, decide whether the verb should be positive or negative according to the text.
   (i) Long-term smoke damage to a property will/will not be paid for.
   (ii) Fences hit by falling trees will/will not be paid for.
   (iii) Damage to your house caused by an overflowing river will/will not be paid for.
   (iv) Damage caused to a roof by heavy snow will/will not be paid for.

(v) If a guest in your house steals something from you, this will/will not be paid for.
(vi) If something is stolen from your house while your whole family is away for two weeks, this will/will not be paid for.
(vii) If you and your family return home after being abroad for three months and find the boiler has leaked and damaged a floor, this will/will not be paid for.
(viii) When your house was built, some of the bricks were of bad quality so one wall has now collapsed. This policy will/will not pay for this.
(ix) Part of a concrete floor in your house has been damaged. Nothing else in or under your house was damaged at the same time. This policy will/will not pay for damage to the floor.
(x) A crack develops in your swimming pool. At the same time a wall of the garage also cracks. The cause of both of these problems seems to be the same. This policy will/will not pay for the damage to both things.

4. A person wants to know what 'additional cover' is provided by this building insurance policy (see Section B). How would the insurance sales representative trying to sell this policy answer the following questions, according to the text? Identify the lines in the policy where you find your answers.

Customer's questions

(i) 'If a pipe in my house leaks becaust it is rusty will you compensate me?'
(ii) 'Will you pay for damage to both inside and outside pipes due to bad weather?
(iii) 'Will you pay for damage to any cable providing a service to my house?'
(iv) 'If my son breaks our window by kicking his football against it, will you pay for it?'
(v) 'If we need to consult lawyers when we make a claim in relation to this policy, will you pay their fees?'
(vi) 'If, after earthquake damage to my house, my local authority requires me to repair one of my buildings, will you repay me?'
(vii) 'If I rent my house to someone else and my house becomes so badly damaged that I can't rent it any more, will you compensate me?'
(viii) 'If I buy a new house which is 10% more expensive than my present one, will this policy cover it completely?'

Vocabulary

5. (a) Look at how the words and phrases in the box below are used in the text and make sure you understand their meaning.

Civil Commotion (line 6)	Heave (line 27)
Collision (line 7)	incurred (line 67)
Vandalism (line 19)	reinstatement (line 70)
Malicious Acts (line 19)	comply (line 71)

(b) Complete the following sentences using the correct word or phrase from the box (in the appropriate grammatical form).

(i) Some insurance companies have __________ losses this year due to bad management.

(ii) After the earthquake there was __________ among the population until the government restored order.

(iii) __________ this staircase in its original style will be very expensive.

(iv) Before you can drive a car it is necessary to __________ with laws regarding insurance.

(v) After the __________ between my car and a bus, my vehicle was a write-off.

(vi) __________ against public property, such as telephones, costs the economy a lot each year.

(vii) As the volcano began to become active, its sides started to __________ outwards.

(viii) As a result of her __________ against the company, she was dismissed.

Text 6.2 Settlement of claims and liability damage

Skim and scan

What is the maximum amount this insurance policy will pay for any one case of death or destruction of property where the person who holds this policy is legally liable?

BASIS OF CLAIMS OF SETTLEMENT

1 We will pay the cost incurred in reinstatement or repair of that part of the buildings which is damaged by any of the causes insured by this section without any deduction for wear and tear provided that at the time of such damage the buildings are in a good state of repair

2 If the damage to the buildings is not reinstated or repaired or the buildings are not in a good state of repair then we will pay at our option

a) the cost of reinstating the damage less a deduction for any wear and tear or betterment, or

b) the difference between the sale value of your home in the open market immediately prior to the damage and its residual value following such damage

3 The most we will pay for any one claim will be the total sum insured shown in the schedule plus any amount payable under paragraphs B5, B6 and B7 of this section

4 The sum insured will not be reduced by a claim payment

5 Any claim settlement for loss or damage will be reduced by the amount of any excess shown in the schedule

YOUR LIABILITY AS PROPERTY OWNER

We will pay all sums for which you become legally liable arising solely from your ownership of your home and its land or from any private dwelling previously owned and occupied by you for accidental

a) death of or bodily injury to any person
b) loss of or damage to material property

occurring during the period of insurance shown in the schedule

but not liability

i) for death of or bodily injury to any member of your family or domestic staff
ii) for damage to property belonging to or in the custody or control of you, your family or domestic staff
iii) arising from
    1) any profession, business or employment
    2) an agreement unless that liability would have existed otherwise

Any claim payment resulting from one incident will not be more than £1,000,000

We will also pay costs, expenses and legal fees necessarily incurred with our written consent.

Specimen Home Insurance Policy, Direct Line Insurance

Text organisation

1. Below are the main points of the text, but in the wrong order. Number them in their correct order according to the text.

	Main points in text	Order
(i)	Any claim paid does not decrease the sum insured.	
(ii)	There is a calculable limit to how much will be paid for one claim.	
(iii)	Deaths and property damage for which you are legally liable will be paid, with certain exceptions.	
(iv)	There is a monetary limit to how much will be paid for one claim.	
(v)	Compensation for unrepaired damage or damage to unrepaired buildings will be calculated in one of two ways.	
(vi)	The full replacement cost of any building in good condition will be paid.	

Comprehension

2. Use one element from box A and one from box B and connect them with the conjunction 'if' to make four sentences which are true according to the text.

A		B
(i) Any charge required to repair a building will be paid	if	(a) the damage itself is not paid for.
(ii) The insurance company can pay part of a building's damage		(b) it was maintained in a good condition
(iii) The loss in sales value from damage will be paid		(c) a claim is made under this policy.
(iv) The amount of your cover is not reduced		(d) it was not well kept when repaired.

3. Look at the situations listed below the chart. In some of these cases, according to the text, the insurance company will pay and in some it will not. Using the text, decide where each situation belongs in the chart. Identify the lines in the text where you find your answers.

Insurance company must pay	Insurance company need not pay

(i) Your housekeeper drops an expensive vase which she is cleaning outside.
(ii) You sign an agreement with an accommodation agency that you will be legally liable if a person to whom you rent a room has an accident in your home.
(iii) A guest falls down your stairs and breaks a leg.
(iv) You are a freelance journalist and you work from home. Your personal computer overheats and causes a fire.
(v) You run a franchise business from your home. You sign an agreement with the company that gave you the franchise that if the fax machine they supplied to you is damaged in your home you will be legally liable for it.
(vi) Your son falls down your stairs and breaks his leg.
(vii) Your ten-year-old daughter's computer has an electrical fault and causes a fire.
(viii) You take a picture home from your art gallery to show to clients who come to your house one evening. It is stolen from your house.
(ix) A guest's handbag is stolen while she is at a party in your house.

Vocabulary

4. The vocabulary used in insurance policies is formal and legalistic. Look at how the words on the left are used in the text and then match them with their more informal equivalents.

Word in text		Informal equivalent	
(a)	incurred (line 1)	(i)	remaining
(b)	reinstatement (line 1)	(ii)	responsible
(c)	option (line 6)	(iii)	only
(d)	betterment (line 8)	(iv)	return to previous condition
(e)	prior to (line 10)	(v)	improvement
(f)	residual (line 10)	(vi)	choice
(g)	settlement (line 16)	(vii)	event
(h)	liable (line 18)	(viii)	payment
(i)	arising (line 18)	(ix)	before
(j)	solely (line 18)	(x)	legal control
(k)	occupied (line 20)	(xi)	caused by
(l)	material property (line 22)	(xii)	agreement
(m)	custody (line 27)	(xiii)	resulting from
(n)	incident (line 33)	(xiv)	physical things
(o)	consent (line 36)	(xv)	lived in

Text 6.3 Conditions which apply to the whole policy

Skim and scan

(a) How soon should a person tell the insurance company when he/she wants to make a claim?

(b) If the insurance company cancels this policy, how much warning of cancellation must they give?

CLAIMS CONDITIONS WHICH APPLY TO THE WHOLE POLICY

1 Notification of a Claim

When you become aware of a claim or potential claim under this policy you must give us notice in writing as soon as reasonably possible

2 Loss or Damage Claims

For any loss or damage claim you must

a) at your expense provide us with such information and evidence as we may request including written estimates and proof of ownership or value

b) notify the police immediately of any loss or damage by deception, theft, attempted theft, vandalism, malicious acts, riot or civil commotion or if any property has been lost outside your home

3 Liability Claims

For any liability claim you must

a) send us any letter, claim, writ or summons in connection with the claim or potential claim immediately it is received

b) not admit, deny, negotiate or settle a claim without our written consent

4 Abandonment

No property may be abandoned to us

5 Enforcing your Rights

We may at our expense and in your name take any steps necessary to enforce your rights against any other person either before or after we pay a claim

6 Other Insurances

If there is any other insurance covering the same loss, damage or liability we will only pay our proportionate share

CONDITIONS WHICH APPLY TO THE WHOLE POLICY

1 Policy Terms and Conditions

You and any other person entitled to benefit under this policy must comply with its terms and conditions

2 Prevention of Loss

You must take all reasonable steps to
a) prevent loss, damage or accident
b) maintain the insured property in sound condition and good repair

3 Cancellation

a) You may cancel the policy by giving us notice in writing and we will make a refund of premium paid for any unexpired period of insurance unless a claim has been made during the current period of insurance
b) We may cancel the policy by sending seven days notice by letter to your last known address when we will make a refund of the premium paid for any unexpired period of insurance
c) If the premium is payable by monthly instalments and payment ceases we will give you seven days notice as provided in paragraph b) above.

Specimen Home Insurance Policy, Direct Line Insurance

Comprehension

1. Say whether the following statements are true or false according to the text. Identify the lines in the text where you find your answers.
   (i) The insurance company will pay for arranging estimates and proof of ownership documents for loss and damage claims.
   (ii) The police should be told at once when an item has been stolen or mislaid outside your house.
   (iii) If you are accused of being liable for damages by another person, you must pass on the document making that claim to your insurer straight away.
   (iv) You can dispute a claim against you before you notify your insurer.

(v) It is not possible for the insurance company to act in your name without first receiving your consent.

(vi) This insurance company will pay the total amount of any loss even if it is also covered by another insurance company.

2. Look at the part of the text headed 'Conditions which apply to the whole policy' (lines 24–39) and complete the following sentences so that they are correct. Be careful with the grammar of your answers.
   (i) Only those who fulfil the terms and conditions of this policy ...
   (ii) In order for property to be covered by this policy, the owner must ...
   (iii) If you have not made a claim on this insurance policy and you cancel it in writing ...
   (iv) If you are paying for this policy by monthly payments and these payments stop ...

Definition	Word(s) in text
Lines 1–18	
(i) possible	
(ii) inform	
(iii) probable costs	
(iv) tricking/cheating	
(v) legal documents (two answers)	
(vi) given over	
(vii) put into effect	
Lines 19–39	
(viii) percentage	
(ix) having the right	
(x) obey	
(xi) keep	
(xii) remaining	
(xiii) stops	

Unit 7 Reinsurance: insuring the insurers

The first text looks at the methods of reinsurance which are available to reinsure property and potential liability claims. The second text looks at how the reinsurance industry has recently been faced with very large claims and how it has responded to this situation.

Text 7.1 Reinsurance in property and liability insurance

Pre-reading

Why do insurers need to reinsure themselves? Who could provide this reinsurance? If reinsurance companies have to pay out large amounts on claims, who in the end provides this money?

Skim and scan

(a) Below are the headings of the three main sections of the text. Identify them as Headings A, B and C.

- (i) Excess-loss treaty
- (ii) Quota share treaty
- (iii) Surplus treaty

Reinsurance in property and liability insurance

1 There are two essential ways in which risk is shared under reinsurance agreements in the field of property and liability insurance. The reinsurance agreement may require the reinsurer to share in every loss that occurs to a reinsured risk, or it may require the reinsurer to pay only after a loss reaches a certain size. Quota share treaties and surplus treaties fall in the first category, while excess-loss treaties comprise the second.

• HEADING A

2 Under a quota share treaty, the *direct-writing company and the reinsurance company agree to share the amount of each risk on some percentage basis. Thus, the ABC Mutual Insurance Company (the direct writer) may have a 50% quota share treaty with the DEF Reinsurance Company (reinsurer). Under such an agreement, the DEF Reinsurance Company will pay 50% of any losses arising from those risks subject to the reinsurance treaty. In return the ABC

Mutual Insurance Company will pay the DEF Reinsurance Company 50% of the premiums it receives from the insureds (with a reasonable allowance made to ABC for the agent's *commission and other expenses connected with putting the business on the books).

• **HEADING B**

3 Under a surplus treaty, the reinsurer agrees to accept some amount of insurance on each risk in excess of a specified net retention. Normally, the amount the reinsurer is obligated to accept is referred to as a number of "lines" and is expressed as some multiple of the retention. A given treaty might specify a net retention of $10,000, with five "lines." Under such a treaty, if the direct writer writes a $10,000 policy, no reinsurance is involved, but the reinsurer will accept the excess of policies over $10,000 up to $50,000. These treaties may be "first-surplus treaties," "second-surplus," and so on. A second-surplus treaty fits over a first-surplus treaty, assuming any excess of the first treaty, and so on for a third or fourth treaty. To illustrate, let us assume that the ABC Mutual Insurance Company (the direct writer), has a first-surplus treaty with a $10,000 net retention and five lines with the DEF Reinsurance Company and a second-surplus treaty with the GHI Reinsurance Company, also with five lines. If ABC sells a $100,000 policy, it must, under the terms of both agreements, retain $10,000. The DEF Reinsurance Company will then assume $50,000 and GHI will assume $40,000:

ABC Mutual Insurance Company $10,000
DEF Reinsurance Company 50,000
GHI Reinsurance Company 40,000

Any loss under this policy would be shared on the basis of the amount of total insurance each company carries. Thus, ABC would pay 10% of any loss, DEF would pay 50%, and GHI would pay 40%. The premium would be divided in the same proportion, again with a reasonable allowance from the reinsurers to the direct writer for the expense of putting the policy on the books.

• **HEADING C**

4 Under an excess-loss treaty, the reinsurer is bound to pay only when a loss exceeds a certain amount. In essence, an excess-loss treaty is simply an insurance policy that has a large deductible taken out by the direct writer. The excess-loss treaty may be written to cover a specific risk or to cover many risks suffering loss from a single occurrence. Such a treaty might, for example, require the reinsurer to pay after the direct-writing company had sustained a loss of $10,000 on a specific piece of property, or it might require payment by the reinsurer if the direct writer suffered loss in excess of $50,000 from any one occurrence. There is, of course, a designated maximum limit of liability for the reinsurer.

'Fundamentals of Risk and Insurance,' Vaughan, E. J., 4th edn (John Wiley, 1986), abridged

Text organisation

1. Use the following five headings to complete the table below in relation to property and liability reinsurance.
   - (i) Surplus treaties
   - (ii) Reinsurer pays above a certain size of loss
   - (iii) Excess loss treaties
   - (iv) Quota share treaties
   - (v) Reinsurer shares in every loss

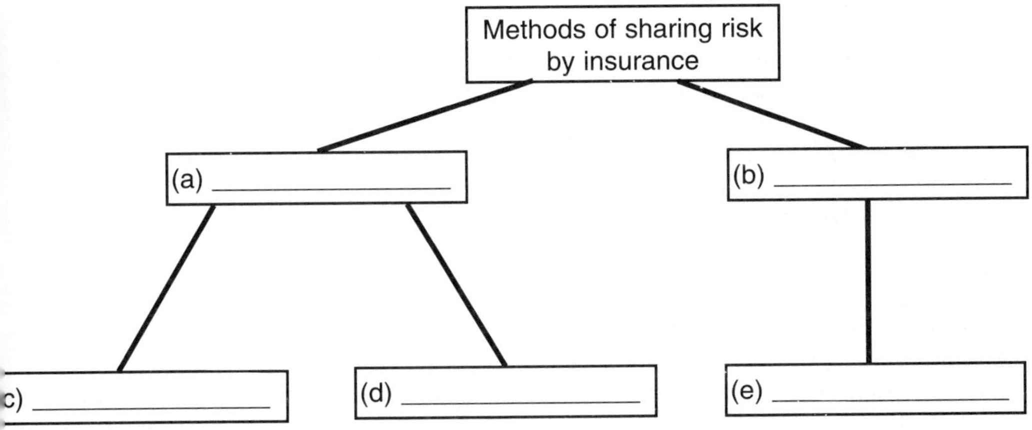

Comprehension

2. On the right below are statements about different types of reinsurance agreement. Identify the type of reinsurance agreement which each statement refers to. Some statements could refer to more than one type of agreement.

Type of reinsurance agreement	Statement
(i) Quota share treaty	(a) There is a maximum amount of liability for the reinsurer. (b) Reinsurer only pays when loss is higher than agreed figure. (c) Most similar to a normal insurance policy. (d) Initial insurer keeps part of premium for sales/admin costs. (e) Each risk is shared on a percentage basis by direct writer and reinsurer.
(ii) Surplus treaty	(f) Can cover a single stated risk or many risks caused by a single event. (g) Requires reinsurer to pay each time except when loss is below a certain amount.
(iii) Excess loss treaty	(h) Premium received by reinsurer corresponds to percentage of possible loss accepted.

3. If insurance company X has a 60% quota share treaty with reinsurance company Y,
   (a) what percentage of any future loss will companies X and Y pay?
   (b) how much of the insurance premium will companies X and Y each receive?
   (c) will Y, receive more or less than the premium figure stated for (b)? Why?

4. (a) With a surplus treaty agreement, what is the name for the amount of any loss which the initial insurer will pay entirely by himself?
   (b) What is the name of any loss which a reinsurer must accept under a surplus treaty agreement?
   (c) What is the relationship between your answers to 4(a) and 4(b)?

5. Alpha Insurance has a first surplus treaty reinsurance agreement with Beta Reinsurance and a second surplus treaty agreement with Gamma Reinsurance. If the net retention figure is $25,000 and both surplus agreements are for six lines,
   (a) how will a claim payout for $250,000 be divided between the three companies?
   (b) how would the premium for this $250,000 insurance arrangement have been divided between the three companies?

6. In the paragraph below, choose the correct alternatives according to the text.

   A reinsurer in an excess-loss treaty (does not have to/has to) pay when a loss is greater than an agreed amount. An excess-loss treaty (is/is not) similar to an ordinary insurance policy which (has/does not have) a large portion of the loss covered by the initial insurer. An excess-loss treaty (can/cannot) cover more than a single risk. There (is/is not) a limit to the liability of the reinsurer with such a treaty.

Vocabulary

7. Look at how the words on the left are used in the text and make sure you understand their meaning. Then match the words to their correct definitions.

Word(s) in text	Definition
(i) quota (line 5)	(a) agreements
(ii) treaties (line 5)	(b) accepts
(iii) fall in (line 5)	(c) measure of accepted loss
(iv) comprise (line 6)	(d) suffered
(v) direct writing (line 7)	(e) arithmetic percentage
(vi) subject to (line 12)	(f) agreed unshared loss
(vii) putting the business on the books (lines 15–16)	(g) first part
(viii) specified net retention (line 18)	(h) covered by
(ix) lines (line 19)	(i) initial insurer
(x) multiple (line 20)	(j) gaining the insurance client
(xi) carries (line 37)	(k) come into
(xii) in essence (line 42)	(l) basically
(xiii) deductible (line 43)	(m) proportion
(xiv) sustained (line 46)	(n) form

Text organisation

8. Below is the next paragraph of the article with some sections removed. Fill in the blanks by choosing from the list that follows. Then write out the whole paragraph.

   Still another method of reinsurance is (i) __________ to that used in aviation insurance under the (ii) __________ of every risk written by a member of the (iii) __________ quota share treaty. On the other hand, the pool (iv) __________ insurance company from a single loss, as is the (v) __________ Bureau. After a member of the pool has (vi) __________ (e.g. £100,000 as a result of one disaster) the (vii) __________ of the loss.

   (a) other members of the pool share the remainder
   (b) case with the Workmens' Compensation Reinsurance
   (c) pooling. The pooling arrangement may be similar
   (d) pool. This pooling arrangement is similar to a
   (e) suffered a loss in excess of a specified amount
   (f) may provide a maximum loss limit to any one
   (g) terms of which each member assumes a percentage

Text 7.2 Insurers get that sinking feeling

Skim and scan

(a) Which are the biggest reinsurance companies in the world?
(b) What was the second-biggest insurance loss ever?

Insurers get that sinking feeling

WHETHER insurers have hearts is debatable. But if they do, the date of August 24th 1992 is surely etched indelibly upon them. That was the day that Hurricane Andrew blew its way through Florida and Louisiana and into the record books, leaving insurers with a repair bill of over $15 billion. Reinsurers – sellers of insurance to insurers – ended up footing much of that bill. As a result, they swore that they would introduce discipline into an industry notorious for relying on gut instinct rather than *actuarial tables. Notably, there would be a re-think of traditional underwriting methods. Two years on, however, little has changed.

2 At first, the hurricane provoked a mini-revolution. The price of catastrophe insurance soared: rates in the end-1992 renewal season were anywhere from 50% to 200% higher than those a year earlier. Retentions, which show the potential losses to which primary insurers opt to stay exposed rather than buying reinsurance, also rose sharply.

3 Why? One reason was that the market's capacity to cover losses had shrunk. Hurricane Andrew followed several years of heavy losses. For several smaller reinsurers, it proved the last straw; they quit the industry. Even the world's two biggest reinsurance firms, Munich Re and Swiss Re, which had previously competed for market share, said that they would turn down business that did not meet tough underwriting criteria. At the same time, capacity at Lloyd's, London's troubled insurance market, was squeezed as "names" – the individuals whose capital supports the market – resigned in droves.

4 Another reason that rates rose was that Hurricane Andrew had caused firms to revise their forecasts of future catastrophes. Munich Re, in particular, talked gloomily about global warming and the fear that it would lead to many more violent storms. To cover the increased probability of higher pay-outs, reinsurers began to charge more for their services.

5 Recently, these trends have gone into reverse, for several reasons. First, 1993 turned out to be a much better year for reinsurers than anyone had

expected, with claims totalling a mere $12 billion. (The bulk of the cost of that year's biggest disaster, the floods in America's Mid-west, fell on the government, not the insurance industry.) As reinsurers turned in bumper results, talk of global warming faded.

Second, reinsurance capacity began to rise again. Lloyd's of London was boosted by the prospect of an injection of capital from newly authorised corporate investors. And Bermuda, hitherto known only as a base for captive insurers (subsidiaries set up to allow industrial firms to insure themselves), suddenly became a force to be reckoned with. The creation of several new firms since November 1992 has boosted the capacity of the island's reinsurers from almost nothing to around $7 billion.

New capacity has not stopped talk of an insurance crisis in Florida and, since January's earthquake in Los Angeles (the second-biggest insured loss ever), in California. Reinsurers have realised that potential catastrophic losses in those states are now so huge that it might never make sense to provide full coverage, reckons Peter Kellogg of A.M. Best, an American firm of insurance analysts. If thousands of homes are not to be left without cover, the government might have to step in. One way it could do so is by selling reinsurance, as proposed by the National Disaster Coalition, a lobby group.

'The Economist', 20 August 1994

Comprehension

1. Here are four summaries of the text. Which one do you think most fully and accurately expresses the main ideas of the text?

   (a) On August 24th 1992 Hurricane Andrew caused 15 billion dollars' worth of damage. As a result of this heavy damage, catastrophe insurance premiums rose by between 50% and 200%. 1993 was a better year for reinsurers, however, as there were only 12 billion dollars' worth of claims. And even the claims for the worst disaster, which was the floods in the Mid-west of America, were mostly paid for by the United States government.

   (b) 1992 was a terrible year for reinsurers due to the big claims caused by Hurricane Andrew, which struck Florida and Louisiana. Florida was so badly affected, as was California when an earthquake struck there, that some people think that it will never be possible to insure those states completely again. One suggestion as to how this problem could be solved, put forward by the National Disaster Coalition, is for the government to become a provider of reinsurance.

   (c) When Hurricane Andrew caused massive insurance costs for reinsurers, they stated that they intended to reform the business. Despite the fact that initially reinsurance premiums did rise sharply, after two years the situation returned to what it had been before Hurricane Andrew. This was because the year after the hurricane was a good one for the reinsurance business, with low claims and an increase in world-wide insurance capacity particularly at Lloyd's of London and in Bermuda.

   (d) Following Hurricane Andrew in 1992 the reinsurance industry completely reorganised its structure and method of doing business. Lloyd's has ceased to be of much importance in the reinsurance industry, its place having been taken by the Bermudan reinsurance companies. Likewise, Munich Re and Swiss Re have largely given up insuring against catastrophes. This is particularly because global warming is now considered sure to produce many more storms Reinsurance premiums, therefore, look likely to remain high.

Text organisation

2. As you saw in an earlier unit (Unit 2, Text 2, question 5), conjunctions and other linking words and phrases are very important in showing the logical relationship between ideas in a text. For further practice in this, look at how the linkers below are used in the text. Then use each of them once only to complete the sentences, paying careful attention to the grammar.

whether (line 1)	that (line 31)
as a result (lines 8–9)	that (line 36)
rather than (line 11)	as (line 50)
notably (line 11)	hitherto (line 57)
even (line 27)	if (line 72)

(i) _________ of the sinking of the Titanic by an iceberg, ships now cross the Atlantic further south.

(ii) My car insurance premium will go up next year _________ I cause an accident this year.

(iii) The government takes money from your earnings for a state pension _________ or not you want one.

(iv) Private health insurance is important in some countries, _________ the United States.

(v) _________ young drivers have to pay more for car insurance is due to their greater chance of having an accident.

(vi) Private medical insurance premiums have _________ risen by more than the rate of inflation.

(vii) Medical malpractice claims are so common in America that _________ very good surgeons are worried about doing operations there.

(viii) Pension funds would normally prefer to receive a lower rate of interest _________ invest in too risky shares.

(ix) The auto insurance policy _________ I took out only covers me against third party damage, fire and theft.

(x) _________ the number of burglaries has increased, household insurance premiums have risen.

Comprehension

3. Find the correct figure in the text for each of the items listed below.

Item	Correct figure
(i) Present reinsurance capacity of Bermuda	
(ii) Amount of damage done by Hurricane Andrew	
(iii) Total amount of 1993 reinsurance claims	
(iv) Year-end percentage increase of catastrophe insurance rates in 1992	

4. Several organisations and places are mentioned in the text. Match the statements on the right to the organisations and places on the left. According to the text, some statements are true about more than one organisation and some companies are referred to by more than one statement. Identify the lines in the text where you find your answers.

Organisation or place		Statement	
(i)	Florida	(a)	One of the world's biggest reinsurers.
(ii)	Louisiana	(b)	Suffered a loss of capital from individuals leaving.
(iii)	Munich Re	(c)	Proposes US government selling reinsurance.
(iv)	Swiss Re	(d)	Biggest disaster in 1993 occurred here.
(v)	Lloyd's	(e)	Where Hurricane Andrew caused most damage.
(vi)	American Mid-west	(f)	Say full insurance for California/Florida may disappear.
(vii)	Bermuda	(g)	Receiving capital from corporate sources.
(viii)	California	(h)	Became an important reinsurer in 1993.
(ix)	A.M. Best	(i)	Second-biggest insurance claim occurred here.
(x)	National Disaster Coalition	(j)	Thought global warming would cause more storms.

5. Referring to the text, put the following events in the order in which they actually occurred. Number the earliest event 1 and the most recent 8.

	Event	Order
(i)	Floods occurred in America's Mid-west.	
(ii)	Talk of an insurance crisis in California began.	
(iii)	Hurricane Andrew devastated Florida and Louisiana.	
(iv)	A number of small reinsurers left the industry	
(v)	Reinsurers promised to reform their industry.	
(vi)	The cost of catastrophe reinsurance and the amount of retentions greatly increased.	
(vii)	Claims for reinsurance came to $12 billion.	
(viii)	An earthquake occurred in Los Angeles.	

Vocabulary

6. Surprisingly, in articles in serious publications like *The Economist* and *The Financial Times* quite colloquial language is used. For non-native speakers, these colloquial expressions are often more difficult to understand than more formal equivalents. Try to understand how the informal words and expressions below are used in the text. Then match them to their more formal equivalents on the right.

Informal word/expression		Formal equivalent	
(i)	footing (line 8)	(a)	be rational
(ii)	gut instinct (line 11)	(b)	unbearable
(iii)	the last straw (lines 26–27)	(c)	intervene
(iv)	squeezed (line 34)	(d)	excellent
(v)	in droves (line 35)	(e)	majority
(vi)	bulk (line 48)	(f)	in great numbers
(vii)	bumper (line 51)	(g)	intuitive feeling
(viii)	injection (line 55)	(h)	taking responsibility for
(ix)	make sense (lines 69–70)	(i)	subject to pressure
(x)	step in (line 74)	(j)	added quantity

Viewpoint

In Text 7.2 it was suggested that the American government should provide reinsurance against major catastrophes if private insurers cannot afford to do so. Do you think this is a good idea? Should the taxpayer in New York, for example, have to provide money to pay for earthquakes in California or hurricanes in Florida? Is there any other solution to this problem?

Unit 8 Risk management and insurance

The first text looks at the question of risk management in general and describes its various elements. The second text looks more specifically at the role of insurance in risk management. It also shows how an insurance company practises risk management itself.

Text 8.1 A risk management program

Pre-reading

What do you think are the elements in a risk management program? What risks do you think it is and is not possible to insure against?

Skim and scan

(a) What are the two main types of risk, according to the text?
(b) Apart from insurance, how many ways are there of coping with potential losses?

A risk management program

1 The scientific method of planning to deal with losses is called risk management. A risk management program usually involves three steps:

1. Identifying and measuring exposures to loss
2. Developing and implementing plans to deal with potential losses after they have been identified
3. Regularly reevaluating and updating the risk management program

Identifying and measuring exposures

2 The recognition that a problem exists is always the first step in solving the problem. Recognizing one's exposure to loss requires organized thinking about the subject. One starting point is to categorize the sources of loss into speculative or pure risk exposures. *Speculative risks* are exposures that can result in gains or losses and usually are not the subject of risk management. Losses or gains that result from bad or good management decisions, from a competitor's actions, or from government intervention in the economy are examples of speculative risks, and these are usually outside the scope of the risk manager's responsibility. Price fluctuations in *commodities or foreign currencies, however, can result in gain or loss, and this speculative risk can be managed with a hedging program.

3 On the other hand, *pure risks* can result only in losses and usually arise from the following sources:

1. Direct losses of property
2. Indirect losses of income because normal business activity has been interrupted by a direct loss
3. Liability losses
4. Losses due to death or disability of key personnel

These pure risks usually can be managed once they have been identified and measured. Regarding measurement, it is well to remember that, before a loss occurs, measurement is merely an estimate. Not all preloss estimates will necessarily reflect with accuracy the actual amount of damages or even the actual amount of exposure to loss.

Developing and implementing a risk management program

4 After all potential sources of loss have been identified and measured, it is the job of the risk manager to develop and implement plans to deal with the potential losses before they occur. Accomplishing this task demands a knowledge of the alternative methods of dealing with risk, the uncertainty about loss. In addition to insurance, six other methods of dealing with potential losses are:

1. Risk avoidance
2. Risk assumption
3. Self-insurance
4. Loss prevention
5. Loss reduction
6. Risk transfer other than insurance

A thorough risk management program is the result of the consideration of all these alternatives rather than the reliance on just one method of dealing with an exposure to loss. In every case the risk manager will carefully weigh the ratio of the costs of a particular risk management approach with the potential benefits to be produced. Since unlimited budgets for risk management are not the rule, spending priorities must be established. Also determining the choice of an appropriate tool are an estimate of the chance of loss and an estimate of the severity of a potential loss.

5 Once a decision has been made to treat an exposure to loss with a given risk management tool, the decision must be implemented. For example, if it has been decided to purchase insurance, arrangements must be made to acquire the proper amount of insurance at the best possible price accompanied by all the service needed or desired. Equally important, once the insurance is in force, the risk manager must be familiar with the terms of the contract so that none of the firm's actions cause the coverage to be suspended or the conditions of the contract to be breached in any way either before or after a loss occurs.

6 If a loss prevention program is decided upon, the risk manager must see to it that all affected employees know what the plan's aims are and what part they are expected to play in the program. The risk manager must remain alert to any advances in safety engineering that may make a given operation or plant or store a safer place in which to work.

'Introduction to Insurance', Dorfman, Mark S. (3rd edn, Prentice Hall 1987), amended

Text organisation

1. Below on the left are the main ideas of the paragraphs 1–6, but in the wrong order. Identify the paragraph that each statement refers to.

	Main idea of paragraph	Paragraph number
(i)	The cost of a risk and its likelihood of occurring determine the method of handling potential losses.	
(ii)	Those risks which only produce losses are called pure risks and must be estimated.	
(iii)	There are several elements in a risk management program.	
(iv)	Most risks which can produce a profit or a loss are not part of the risk manager's job.	
(v)	Risk management requires full staff co-operation and attention to new safety developments.	
(vi)	The efficient and legally correct use of chosen risk management tools is essential.	

Comprehension

2. (a) The text mentions three steps which are normally part of a risk management program. From the six actions described below, choose the three which are mentioned in the text. Identify lines in the text where you find your answers.
   (i) Carry out an evaluation of all the property in a company.
   (ii) Continue to monitor the effectiveness of a risk management program.
   (iii) Decide which potential losses to deal with.
   (iv) Work out how to handle losses that may occur.
   (v) Decide where potential losses may occur and calculate their value.
   (vi) Eliminate all possibilities of potential losses occurring.

   (b) Decide in what order the actions you chose for 2(a) should be carried out, according to the text.

3. Below are some descriptions and examples of risks. Mark those which refer to speculative risk 'SR', and those which refer to pure risk 'PR'.

	Description/ example	Type of risk	Line numbers
(i)	Can only result in a loss.		
(ii)	Managing director of company dies.		
(iii)	Quality of management decisions.		
(iv)	Can result in profit or loss.		
(v)	Competitor goes out of business.		
(vi)	Because of fire at factory, January sale is cancelled.		
(vii)	Price of coffee beans in Brazil rises sharply.		
(viii)	Company is sued because of injury to a worker.		

4. Listed below are the seven methods of dealing with potential losses. Match the method on the left with the appropriate example on the right.

Method of dealing with losses		Example of method	
(i)	Insurance	(a)	A company forms a subsidiary to provide it with insurance.
(ii)	Risk avoidance	(b)	A building lease includes a cancel option for outdated building.
(iii)	Risk assumption	(c)	A company does not invest in a country where war is likely.
(iv)	Self-insurance	(d)	An automatic fire sprinkler is installed in a warehouse.
(v)	Loss prevention	(e)	A Los Angeles firm arranges compensation in case of an earthquake.
(vi)	Loss reduction	(f)	A safety officer is employed to minimise staff injuries.
(vii)	Risk transfer other than insurance	(g)	A company decides to bear the possible loss of small tools.

5. Finish the following sentences with the ending that is correct according to the text.
   (a) When organising a risk management program,
      (i) one of the risk management methods will normally be most suitable.
      (ii) it is best to utilise one risk management method only.
      (iii) the value of each risk management method will be considered.
      (iv) all of the risk management methods should be given equal emphasis.
   (b) Factors determining the choice of risk management methods are
      (i) the possibilities of, and estimated size of, any losses that would take place.
      (ii) the certainties that losses will be suffered and that they will be of a given amount.
      (iii) the almost non-existent chances of loss which will, in any case, be small.
      (iv) the requirements of minimising management costs and limiting insurance expenditure.

6. Two methods of risk management are discussed in more detail in the text. Below, identify the two methods at A and B. Then write the two main points which are given about each method in the text.

Risk management method A: ____________
Main points of method: (i) ____________
(ii) ____________

Risk management method B: ____________
Main points of method: (i) ____________
(ii) ____________

Vocabulary

7. Because this passage is taken from a textbook, the language is rather formal. Look at how the words on the left below are used in the text and then match them with their more informal equivalents on the right.

Formal word(s)		Informal equivalent	
(i)	exposures to (line 3)	(a)	modernising
(ii)	implementing (line 4)	(b)	show
(iii)	updating (line 6)	(c)	possibilities of
(iv)	categorize (line 9)	(d)	take into account
(v)	scope (line 14)	(e)	main aims
(vi)	fluctuations (line 15)	(f)	size
(vii)	disability (line 23)	(g)	carrying out
(viii)	reflect (line 27)	(h)	permanent injury
(ix)	thorough (line 40)	(i)	divide
(x)	weigh (line 42)	(j)	broken
(xi)	the rule (line 44)	(k)	range/area
(xii)	priorities (line 45)	(l)	common
(xiii)	severity (line 47)	(m)	careful
(xiv)	breached (line 55)	(n)	changes

Text organisation

8. The sentences of the next paragraph of the text are given below, but in the wrong order. Number them in their correct order. Before doing this exercise, re-read the last paragraph of the main text. Pay particular attention to conjunctions and pronouns in the following sentences, as this will help you with the exercise.

	Sentence	Order
(i)	Or, the decision might have to be revised as other circumstances change.	
(ii)	The risk manager should be satisfied that a decision has been made concerning every potential source of loss, including direct and indirect property losses, liability losses and key personnel losses.	
(iii)	Such a manual allows others to understand such things as what to do in the event of loss, why specific decisions were made, and what steps to follow if a given contingency arises.	
(iv)	Even if a decision is made to do nothing about a particular source of loss, this decision should be noted.	
(v)	In fact, developing a well-written and well-understood statement of risk management principles, procedures and practices is an important function of the risk manager.	
(vi)	It might be desirable to review the decision if a loss occurs.	

Text 8.2 The insurance mechanism

Skim and scan

(a) From what background did many early developers of risk management come?
(b) Does risk management replace the need for insurance?

The insurance mechanism

1 One of the chief problems that risk management has had to overcome has been to differentiate itself from insurance, partly because of the insurance background of many of the pioneers in risk management thinking, and partly because risk – at least those varieties of it with which risk management is chiefly concerned – has for so long been considered the preserve of insurance alone. The confusion has been perpetuated because insurance retains such an important role as the main method of risk financing in a risk management programme.

2 Risk management does not supersede insurance, but puts it in its proper perspective, as fulfilling a useful function determined after critical assessment of what it has to offer compared with other financing possibilities. To get the best out of any risk management programme, therefore, requires a knowledge of how the insurance mechanism works, and an appreciation of ways in which the insurance industry treats the risk passed on to it in return for the premium paid.

3 For the purchaser, insurance provides a method of smoothing loss experience over a period of time, by exchanging the static risk which is insured for the smaller risk of the failure of the insurer to settle a claim when it is made, either through lack of funds or by some breach of the conditions of the insurance contract by the insured himself.

4 Except for the small insured, or the catastrophic loss, it is unlikely that the cost of loss will be permanently transferred from the insured to the insurer; for the latter will seek to recover what he has paid out by increased premiums in subsequent years, or he may already have recovered it in previous years when the premiums paid have been greater than the amount needed to pay claims and meet the insurer's expenses.

5 Where the market for a particular type of risk is not governed by rating agreements between insurers, it may be possible to defer or avoid repayment of the cost of loss by changing insurers, but in most cases this will be only a short-term solution, unless there has been some substantial improvement in loss control to improve the probable future cost of loss. A new insurer may offer a lower premium, taking the chance that the loss experience will improve, but if it does not, then the premium cost is likely to rise to, and perhaps beyond, its old level.

6 The service of chronological loss spreading is, however, what the insured really needs, even if the total cost is not thereby reduced, for it enables him to

reduce the annual cost of large losses to a size at which they can be borne in a single accounting year.

7 From the insurer's point of view, the risk that is transferred to him has a different aspect. What was a static risk for the insured becomes a dynamic risk for the insurer, for in his hands it presents possibilities either of profit or of loss. The fact that a reinsurance market exists as a method of treating this risk is, however, a reminder that static risk and insurable risk are not synonymous terms.

8 The methods the insurer uses to treat the risk he carries are themselves a good example of risk management in action. He seeks first of all to diminish his risk by ensuring that it is well spread. This is achieved in a number of ways. First, a good spread of risk is sought by endeavouring to ensure that the portfolio he is insuring consists of a large number of similar items. This will give the greatest play to the operation of the *law of large numbers, and thus improve the predictability of the loss experience. Next, the insurer will wish these insurances to come from many different locations to provide the necessary geographical spread to minimise the chance of an abnormal loss experience due to a localised catastrophe.

'An Introduction to Risk Management', Crockford, Neil (Woodhead-Faulkner, 1980), amended

Text organisation

1. In the chart below are some of the conjunctions and linking phrases from the text. Look at how they are used in the text and then match them to alternative linkers or expressions on the right which have the same meaning. The alternative you choose should also be grammatically correct when substituted in the text for the original linker.

Conjunction in text	Alternative
(i) because of (line 2)	(a) the reason being that
(ii) therefore (line 12)	(b) in this way
(iii) either ... or (line 18)	(c) in fact
(iv) Except for (line 20)	(d) as a result of
(v) for (line 21)	(e) excluding
(vi) Where (line 26)	(f) the situation that
(vii) unless (line 29)	(g) afterwards
(viii) then (line 32)	(h) with the exception of the case that
(ix) however (line 34)	(i) for that reason
(x) even if (line 35)	(j) because of ... or ...
(xi) What (line 39)	(k) in those conditions when
(xii) thus (line 49)	(l) regardless of whether

Comprehension

2. (a) According to the text, what is one of the main problems for risk management?
   (b) What are the three reasons for the answer to 2(a)?

3. Show whether the author of this text would agree (✓) or disagree (**x**) with the following statements.

Statement	Author's opinion
(i) Risk management replaces insurance.	
(ii) Risk management indicates the role of insurance in relation to other means of risk management.	
(iii) A good risk manager needs to understand well how insurance functions.	
(iv) A risk manager needn't be concerned with a risk after an insurance company accepts it.	

4. Put the following sentences into their logical order according to the text.
   (i) A claim could be unpaid if the insurance company was short of money.
   (ii) The risk of a lot of money being lost at one time can be reduced through insurance.
   (iii) A person could invalidate a claim by not following the requirements of his/her insurance policy.
   (iv) The possibilities of a large one-off loss can be replaced by a smaller risk of default on an insurance claim.

5. Decide whether the statements below are true or false according to the text.

Statement	True/false
(i) In most cases of insurance loss, a loss becomes the permanent cost of the insurer.	
(ii) Where there is true competition between insurers, the insured person can avoid bearing a loss.	
(iii) If new ways of reducing future losses are found, this could prevent past losses having to be paid for by past claimants.	
(iv) New insurers can offer lower rates than their competitors by assuming that future losses will be less than before.	
(v) New insurers can maintain lower rates than competitors even if loss levels in the industry remain the same.	
(vi) The most important thing about insurance for the insured person is that the cost of the total loss is reduced.	
(vii) The insured person regards the division of a large loss into manageable parts as essential.	
(viii) The reinsurance market exists because static risk and insurable risk are the same.	

6. (a) What technique of risk management, used by insurers, is mentioned in the text?
   (b) How many types of that technique are mentioned in the text?
   (c) What are those types of technique, according to the text?

Vocabulary

7. (a) The style of this text is academic and therefore uses rather formal language. Find formal words in the text which are expressed more informally below. The paragraphs where you will find the words are indicated in brackets.

Informal expression	Formal word in text
(i) solve (paragraph 1)	
(ii) belonging to (paragraph 1)	
(iii) keeps (paragraph 1)	
(iv) break (paragraph 3)	
(v) later (paragraph 4)	
(vi) controlled (paragraph 5)	
(vii) delay (paragraph 5)	
(viii) over time (paragraph 6)	
(ix) in this way (paragraph 6)	
(x) interchangeable (paragraph 7)	

(b) The five verbs below from the text are all formal and are important for understanding the text.

differentiate (line 2)	endeavouring (line 55)
has been perpetuated (line 7)	minimise (line 60)
supersede (line 10)	

Look at how these verbs are used in the text. Then use these verbs, in their correct form, to replace the underlined parts of the following sentences.

(i) Insurance companies <u>try</u> to reduce their losses by charging high premiums forvery risky policies.
(ii) Insurance companies <u>distinguish</u> between safe and careless drivers when selling motor insurance.
(iii) Private security firms have, to a large extent, <u>replaced</u> the police as protectors of property.
(iv) Skilled claims investigators are required to <u>reduce as much as possible</u> false insurance claims.
(v) Disease in some countries <u>continues</u> at a high level because of poor sanitation.

Text organisation

8. Below are the next three paragraphs of the text but they are not in the right order. Decide what the correct order is. Before you try this, look at the last paragraph of the main text (i.e. paragraph 8) as this will help you to do this exercise.

(i) In financing his risks, the insurer adopts sound risk management tactics in retaining only that part of the potential loss which can comfortably be borne in a single accounting year. The existence of the reinsurance market, which is designed to provide exactly this service to the direct insurer, makes it simple for him to buy cover for the large and catastrophic risk only.

(ii) This is the classic picture of the insurer as the collector of contributions from many to pay for the losses of the few that suffer them. It is still a true picture for many smaller types of insurances, but the changing nature of risk is reducing its validity for many of the more potentially catastrophic types of risk.

(iii) As well as spreading risk geographically in this way, the insurer also seeks to spread it chronologically, by building up reserves for future losses – a process which is easier in nearly all countries for an insurer than for any other type of company which might like to do the same from its own funds; for an insurer, unlike other companies, is permitted to set up reserves of this kind out of pre-tax earnings. This fact has been one of the attractions of setting up a captive insurance company as part of a risk financing programme.

Unit 9 Insurance organisations

Text 9.1 shows how German banks and insurance companies have created various types of organisation to market each other's products. The second text looks at the circumstances which led Lloyd's of London, probably the most famous insurance company in the world, into severe financial difficulties.

Text 9.1 All aboard for Allfinanz

Pre-reading

The European Economic Community (now the Eurpoean Union) is creating a single market for the sale of insurance. What effect will this have on companies selling or intending to sell insurance in the EEC (EU)? What will be the advantages and disadvantages of this single market for consumers?

Skim and scan

(a) What is *Allfinanz*?
(b) Which insurance company did Deutsche Bank buy?

All aboard for Allfinanz

1 The Germans coined the term *Allfinanz,* the marriage of banking with insurance and other services for retail customers, yet their banks and insurers have lagged behind European rivals in putting it into effect. French banks, for instance, sell 35% of France's life insurance; German banks a puny 5%. But thanks to the EC's single market, Germany's insurance market will be deregulated in 1994. Foreign competition could then threaten the domestic cartels that dominate German insurance. That should force German banks to catch up.

2 Habit, law and the balance of power among financial institutions explain Germany's backwardness. Bankers and insurance agents are not used to selling each other's products. Savers usually buy insurance from agents tied to a single insurer, rather than from banks. The tax authorities encourage segregation by refusing to give tax breaks to types of insurance that mimic banking products. And some banks have been loth to start their own insurance operations lest they offend insurers, which are among their best customers.

So most banks have sought to deliver *Allfinanz* through alliances, a strategy that entails modest costs but also produces modest returns. Allianz, Germany's biggest insurer, co-operates in some areas with Dresdner Bank; in others with Bayerische Hypothekenbank or co-operative banks. Its alliances with Dresdner and Hypobank are cemented by shareholdings; its banking partners sell 17% of its life-insurance policies. Commerzbank owns 48% of its insurance partner DBV and sells DM1 billion ($600m) of DBV's life insurance.

Bolder approaches have not been particularly successful. AMB, Germany's second-biggest insurer, plunged into *Allfinanz* by buying BFG, a former trade-union bank. It lost more than DM750m on BFG's bad loans, and the bank sold less insurance than AMB hoped. AMB has since sold BFG to a French bank (it is itself partly-owned by a French insurer), though it continues to market insurance through BFG branches.

The deregulation of Germany's insurance market in mid-1994 will free prices and allow insurers to experiment with new products. That will drive banks and insurers closer together and may promote mergers and takeovers among companies that now co-operate. One reason is that banks can sell standard life insurance more cheaply than insurers' tied agents. As competition heats up, that price advantage will tell.

A second reason, says Sven-Michael Slottko, a former head of Deutsche Bank's life insurance operation, is that mere allies cannot invent true banking-insurance hybrids without squabbling over how to split the profits. Insurers require high commissions; banks live off spreads. Only a combined *Allfinanz* group, says Mr Slottko, can sell an insurance policy that sacrifices commission for a high spread.

Deutsche Bank's insurance venture may be a sign of things to come. Alone among big banks, Deutsche started its own company, DB Leben, in 1989. In 1992 DB Leben sold DM7.2 billion worth of life insurance through Deutsche's branches, putting it among Germany's top 15 life insurers. Despite this apparent success, Deutsche suddenly abandoned its go-it-alone strategy last year by buying 65% of Deutscher Herold, a medium-sized insurer. Deutsche has since transferred its insurance business to Herold and the insurance men who run it. Hilmar Kopper, Deutsche's chairman, calls the purchase of Herold "the most significant move we have made for years."

'The Economist' 25 September 1993

Text organisation

1. Match each of the following aims with the paragraph it belongs to.

Main aim of paragraph	Paragraph number
(i) Explain the causes of the present German banking-insurance situation.	
(ii) Show why bank and insurance 'alliances' will not work satisfactorily.	
(iii) Describe existing alliances involving German bankers and insurers.	
(iv) Compare banking/insurance relationships in Germany and other countries.	
(v) Outline a specific example of a bank buying an insurer.	
(vi) Show why insurance deregulation will encourage mergers and takeovers.	
(vii) Outline a specific example of an insurer buying a bank.	

Comprehension

2. (a) Who invented the term '*Allfinanz*'?
   (b) What is ironic about this fact?
   (c) What could change the situation which is the answer to 2(b)?

3. (a) How many reasons are there for *Allfinanz* being limited in Germany?
   (b) From the list below of possible reasons for *Allfinanz* being limited in Germany, choose the ones which are stated in the text.
      (i) There are no tax benefits for insurance products which are similar to banking products.
      (ii) Insurance products and banking products are too different.

(iii) It is too costly for banks to sell insurance and vice-versa.
(iv) If banks in Germany sell insurance they might annoy important insurance companies.
(v) There are legal restrictions on banks selling insurance.
(vi) Banks and insurance companies do not know how to market each other's products.
(vii) Foreign banking and insurance companies control too much of the market in Germany.
(viii) Germans are not used to buying insurance from a bank.

4. Does the author think alliance between banks and insurers is a good way to implement *Allfinanz*? What sentence gives you your answer?

5. On the left below are the names of German banks and insurance companies mentioned in the text. Match these to statements on the right.

Company	Statement
(i) Allianz	(a) DM 1 billion of its insurance is sold by Commerzbank
	(b) Still sells AMB insurance
	(c) Was bought by AMB
(ii) DBV	(d) 48% owned by Commerzbank
	(e) Now owned by a French bank
	(f) Had to pay off a bank's bad debt
	(g) Owns shares in Hypobank
(iii) AMB	(h) Expected to sell more insurance than it did
	(i) Second-largest German insurer.
	(j) Co-operates with Bayerische Hypotheken
(iv) BFG	(k) 17% of its life insurance is sold by banks

6. (a) What happened in Germany in mid-1994?
(b) What effect does the author expect this to have on prices and products?
(c) What result would your answer to 6(b) have on the relationship between banks and insurance companies in Germany?

7. Decide whether the statements below are true or false according to the text. Note the lines where you find your answers.

	Statement	True/false	Line numbers
(i)	Life policies are cheaper bought from insurance agents than from banks.		
(ii)	As competition in insurance increases in Germany, price will become more important.		
(iii)	Banks and insurance companies in a loose relationship can easily divide profits.		

(iv) Insurance companies and banks make their profits in different ways.		
(v) *Allfinanz* companies don't find it easier than normal banks and insurance firms to sell insurance profitably.		

8. Below are a number of events described in paragraph 7, but in the wrong order. Number them in their correct order according to the text.

Event	Order
(i) Deutsche Bank handed over insurance management to Deutscher Herold.	
(ii) DB Leben became one of the major life insurance companies in Germany.	
(iii) Deutsche Bank purchased a middle-sized insurance company.	
(iv) Deutsche Bank founded its own insurance company.	

Vocabulary

9. Articles in magazines are not always written in either a completely formal or a completely informal style: they may use vocabulary of both kinds. To see this, mark the following vocabulary from the text 'F' if you think it is formal or 'I' if you think it is informal. Then match the words to their more formal or informal equivalent on the right. The first one has been done for you.

Word in text	Formal/ informal	More informal/ formal equivalent
(i) coined (line 1) →	→ I →	insignificant
(ii) lagged behind (line 4)		small
(iii) puny (line 7)		connected
(iv) backwardness (line 15)		requires
(v) tied (line 17)		gives up
(vi) loth (line 22)		delay
(vii) lest (line 22)		compel
(viii) entails (line 26)		intensifies
(ix) modest (line 26)		disagreeing
(x) plunged into (line 39)		→ invented
(xi) drive (line 49)		not wanting
(xii) heats up (line 54)		suddenly entered
(xiii) squabbling (line 58)		divide
(xiv) split (line 59)		developed more slowly
(xv) sacrifices (line 62)		in case

Text 9.2 Leaking at the seams

Pre-reading

What do you know about the history of Lloyd's? What have you heard about its recent difficulties? Do you know of any steps Lloyd's have taken to try to solve these problems?

Skim and scan

(a) Who is David Coleridge?
(b) Who are Chatset?

Leaking at the seams

1 HAUNTED by catastrophes past, Lloyd's of London faces a bleak future. Some wonder whether, in any recognisable form, by 2000 it will even be there. This matters to more than just those smooth scions of the British upper class who work in this singular insurance market, or to those who pledge their wealth, as *"names", to back the market's *underwriting syndicates. Though this collective of co-operatives pulls in only as much premium income as some of Britain's big insurance companies, Lloyd's is synonymous with British insurance. An enfeebled Lloyd's would harm the *City of London's international standing.

2 It was this thought that held the British government back from putting Lloyd's firmly under its thumb during the fraud-ridden years of the late 1970s and early 1980s. The market has since done much to polish up its self-regulation, though it is still far from squeaky-clean. Today, however, the biggest problem that faces David Coleridge, who took over this month as chairman of Lloyd's, is not one of scandal, but of profits. In the next couple of years these will prove uniformly bad, underscoring the steady loss of competitiveness from which Lloyd's has suffered recently. The market's share of world premium income was 2.2% in 1983, but is only half that today.

3 The latest published figures for Lloyd's show £575m ($950m) of pre-tax profit in 1987 (Lloyd's syndicates close their accounts only after three years), down slightly on the record profits of 1986. That was before a blast of natural and man-made catastrophes in 1988–90 sent insurance claims pouring into Lloyd's: the fire on the Piper Alpha oil platform, the spillage from the *Exxon Valdez*, the San Francisco earthquake, Hurricane Hugo and a spate of European gales. Worse, these disasters coincided with falling premium rates in almost every one of the market's businesses. Today Chatset, an independent consultancy, reckons Lloyd's will post a meagre profit for 1988 and a loss of more than £850m for 1989, the first loss since 1967.

4 Many of the 26,500 names would therefore love to follow the 6,000 who have already shaken the dust of Lloyd's from their feet these past three years. Yet half the names could not leave even if they wanted to: they are locked into the 58 (out of a total of 401) Lloyd's syndicates that have been unable to close one or more of their past annual accounts, so unquantifiable are the liabilities stacking up against them.

5 Many of the resultant 92 "open years" have to do with old American liabilities – for asbestos-related risks, for example, and pollution – whose scale was undreamt-of when the insurance (or, more usually, the reinsurance) policies were underwritten. The most notorious case concerns the 1,600 names on 31 Outhwaite syndicates. These face losses, mainly on asbestosis claims, of up to £1 billion; since Lloyd's names have unlimited liability, many will be bankrupted. A case that looks set to rival Outhwaite in notoriety concerns two Feltrim syndicates, where at least £200m of losses are emerging on "excess-of-loss" insurance in 1987–89.

6 Nor do the market's commercial troubles end there. Other unsuspected "long-tail" claims are now hitting it, notably untold billions of coming dollars for professional negligence. Most visible are the claims arising out of the gross mismanagement during the 1980s of America's savings-and-loan institutions. Open years are proving to be open wounds for Lloyd's.

'The Economist' 26 January 1991

Text organisation

1. Below are the main ideas of the paragraphs 1–6 but they are not in the same order as the text. Match each of the ideas below with its correct paragraph.

	Main idea of paragraph	Paragraph number
(i)	Following several major disasters, Lloyd's profits were likely to turn into losses.	
(ii)	In addition to asbestos and pollution claims, other 'long-tail' claims will badly affect Lloyd's.	
(iii)	Some fear that Lloyd's will not survive to the year 2000, which would damage the City of London's financial reputation.	
(iv)	Many of Lloyd's 'names', wanting to leave Lloyd's, cannot do so because their syndicates still have 'open' accounts.	
(v)	Despite improved internal financial controls, Lloyd's is still not efficient enough and this has weakened its market position.	
(vi)	Because of massive losses on asbestos and pollution policies by some syndicates, many 'names' will face financial ruin.	

2. In previous units (see Text 1.2, question 1 and Text 4.2, question 1) you saw how pronouns and other phrases are used to refer to things mentioned earlier or later in a text. To develop your understanding of this further, find the pronouns or phrases which refer to the following parts of the text. The first one has been done for you.
   (i) 'Lloyd's of London' (lines 1–2) is referred to by <u>'it'</u> in line <u>3</u>.
   (ii) 'whether, in any recognisable form, by 2000 it will even be there' (lines 3–4) is referred to by __________ in line __________ .
   (iii) 'the market's underwriting syndicates' (line 8) are referred to by __________ in line __________ .
   (iv) 'An enfeebled Lloyd's would harm the City of London's international standing' (lines 12–14) is referred to by __________ in line __________ .
   (v) 'the British government' (lines 15–16) is referred to by __________ in line __________ .
   (vi) 'The market' (line 18) is referred to by __________ and __________ in line __________ .
   (vii) 'The market's share of world premium income was 2.2% in 1983' (lines 27–28) is referred to by __________ in line __________ .
   (viii) 'Lloyd's show £575m ($950m) of pre-tax profit in 1987' (lines 30–31) is referred to by __________ in line __________ .
   (ix) 'the fire on the Piper Alpha oil platform, the spillage from the *Exxon Valdez*, the San Francisco earthquake, Hurricane Hugo and a spate of European gales' (lines 36–39) are referred to by __________ in line __________ .

(x) 'half the names' (line 49) are referred to by __________ in line __________ and __________ in line __________.

(xi) 'Lloyd's names' (line 63) are referred to by __________ in line __________ .

Comprehension

3. Many events are mentioned in this text but they are not described in exactly the order in which they occurred. Use the text to number these events (1–9) in their actual time sequence. Where possible, write the date of the events.

Event	Order of events	Date of events
(i) Lloyd's suffered from dishonest activity.		
(ii) Profits bad or non-existent.		
(iii) Lloyd's share of world insurance premium income was 2.2%.		
(iv) Lloyd's share of world insurance premium income is 1.1%.		
(v) Lloyd's made a profit of more than £550 million.		
(vi) Lloyd's made a record profit.		
(vii) Major disasters produced large insurance claims on Lloyd's.		
(viii) The first year of loss for Lloyd's mentioned in text.		
(ix) Syndicates had losses of £200 million on 'excess of loss' insurance.		

4. For each of the sentences below, choose the ending which is true according to the text.
   (a) It is important for Britain for Lloyd's to survive because
      (i) it is supported by private individuals who commit their financial resources to it.
      (ii) it earns so much premium income.
      (iii) it provides employment for members of the British upper class.
      (iv) it is a symbol of London's financial importance.
   (b) Lloyd's profits have fallen recently because
      (i) it is experiencing dishonest activities again as it did in the 1970s and 1980s.
      (ii) it has not kept itself as competitive as other insurance organisations.
      (iii) the demand for insurance world-wide has fallen.
      (iv) it did not do anything to eliminate the illegal practices which started in the 1970s.

5. (a) How long after a particular year do Lloyd's syndicates know if they have made a profit or loss on that year's business?

(b) How many 'names' were there providing finance for Lloyd's three years before this article was written?

6. In what circumstances is it not possible for a Lloyd's account to be closed? What lines in the text tell you this?

7. Below are some figures from the text. Match these figures with the descriptions that follow.

(a) 31	(b) 58	(c) 2	(d) 1,600	(e) 401	(f) 92

(i) The number of Feltrin syndicates expecting heavy losses
(ii) The number of Lloyd's syndicates still with open annual accounts
(iii) The number of names facing losses of £1 billion
(iv) The total number of Lloyd's insurance account years not closed
(v) The total number of syndicates at Lloyd's
(vi) The number of syndicates involved in loss-making asbestos insurance

8. (a) What is the expression used in the text to describe those types of insurance claims at Lloyd's which cannot be closed at the end of an annual account?
(b) Apart from asbestos and pollution, what is another major source of the claims you identified in 8(a)?

Vocabulary

9. The vocabulary in this text is quite difficult but we can divide the problem words into four categories for study.

(a) **Phrasal verbs**
Match the phrasal verb on the left with its correct meaning according to the text.

Phrasal verb	Meaning
(i) pulls in (line 9)	improve
(ii) polish up (line 19)	be in a trap
(iii) are locked into (line 50)	earn
(iv) stacking up against (line 54)	increase

(b) **Hyphenated words**
Explain the meanings of the following hyphenated words as they are used in the text.
(i) fraud-ridden (line 17)
(ii) squeaky-clean (line 20)
(iii) asbestos-related (lines 56–57)

(c) **Metaphors**

There are several metaphors in the text and another in the title. Metaphors are expressions describing one thing in terms of something completely different. For example, 'a busy bee' means a very active or hardworking person. The three metaphors in the text relate to parts of the human body. Find these and match them with their correct meanings below. The paragraph where each metaphor occurs is indicated.

Metaphor	Meaning
(i) paragraph 2 (ii) paragraph 4 (iii) paragraph 6	A source of continued pain. B to supervise an organisation carefully C to have left an organisation

(d) **Other words**

Note how the words in the box are used in the text and then use these words, in their appropriate grammatical form, to complete the sentences below.

Haunted by (line 1)	underscoring (line 25)
bleak (line 2)	spillage (line 37)
scions (line 5)	spate (line 39)
singular (line 6)	meagre (line 44)
pledge (line 7)	notoriety (line 65)
synonymous with (line 12)	notably (line 71)
enfeebled (line 12)	

(i) The future is __________ for those unemployed people who have no skills.
(ii) The company __________ to pay for the pollution it had caused.
(iii) It would __________ the company for its creditors to insist that it pay all its debts immediately.
(iv) He __________ the size of the disaster by saying that the insurance firm couldn't afford to pay for all of the damage.
(v) The fact that the company spent only a __________ amount on fire safety was one cause of the accident.
(vi) There has been a __________ of accidents on that road since its speed limit was increased.
(vii) Lloyd's has contracted some __________ insurance policies over the years, such as the ones protecting film stars' legs.
(viii) The poor __________ of this wealthy family were trying to appear as rich as their older brother.
(ix) __________ of chemicals from factories into rivers is one major form of pollution today.
(x) The __________ of the losses suffered by some Lloyd's 'names' has discouraged people from joining Lloyd's.

1) disposition

ii) defined - contribution plan.

~~plan de prestación~~ definida

3) provisions

4) with respect to

5) defined - distribution plan

6) entity

7) formula

8) elligible.

9) collective - bargaining process.

10) projected.

11) accumulates -

PROFIT - SHARING plan = participación de beneficios

PENSION FUNDS

fondo de pensiones - 18.000

David (MARTES 3)

S. Present
nationalities adjectives
objective pronouns:
a/an/the

Contrast S. Present / Present Continuous.
adverbs of frequency.
routines

I like / I'd like.
Which car do you like? one/ones
c, u / some, any, no.
in/on/at
space prep.

S. Past:

'Clothes.'

- going to / pres. continuous.
- comparative adjectives. / Superlatives

Miriam : fotocopias frases / tests

defined - benefit plan
de prestación definida

defined - contribution
de aportación definida -

trillion

(xi) _________ advances have been made in the treatment of disease in the 20th century.

(xii) The nuclear industry is _________ the disaster at Chernobyl, making it difficult to convince people of its safety.

(xiii) In English 'assassinate' is not _________ with 'murder'.

Viewpoint

What do you think of Lloyd's system of funding their insurance system by relying on the 'unlimited liability' of private individuals?

Do you think that Lloyd's will survive its present crisis?

Unit 10 Insurance marketing

The first text in this unit looks in detail at how an American insurance company found out which potential customers it should focus its sales efforts on. The second text explains how the efforts of American banks to market insurance products are affected by legislation in that country.

Text 10.1 United Group: how an insurance agency generates sales leads

Pre-reading

Should insurance be marketed in the same ways as other services? Which advertising media are the most suitable for selling insurance? How has the creation of 'direct insurance' organisations affected the insurance industry?

Skim and scan

(a) Which publication does United Group use to find new customers?
(b) How much money does United Group expect to save in annual mailing costs as a result of their mathematical model?

United Group: how an insurance agency generates sales leads

1 United Group is an insurance agency selling hospital protection plans to small businesses. Its customers are usually self-employed repairpeople, printers, electricians, and restaurant owners who have one to two employees (including themselves). United Group's yearly sales are $140 million.

2 Company sales agents sell United Group products exclusively and rely on a *one-call close. To keep its sales force of 1,000 + agents busy, the firm needs to generate 750,000 qualified sales leads per year. Such leads are from two sources: one-third come from 15-million mail pieces, and two-thirds come from more than 10-million phone calls. United relies heavily on the lists of small businesses contained in such sources as the *Yellow Pages* and *Dun & Bradstreet New Business*.

3 The firm has set up a sophisticated system to determine the most responsive and profitable population groups contained in these lists. Responsiveness and profitability can be judged on the basis of such criteria as the number of sales made by the field sales force, the amount of business placed, lapses in insurance coverage (and nonrenewals), and claims experience.

4 Through an early mathematical model that it developed, United Group learned the following:

- Among occupational groups, gas station owners are highly profitable prospects; salespeople have sold $1,446 in premiums per 1,000 pieces mailed, 18 per cent above the average for all occupations. In contrast, although consultants have a high response rate, they have yielded only $554 of premiums per 1,000 pieces mailed.
- Among geographical areas, North Carolina residents have yielded an average of $2,080 in premiums per 1,000 pieces mailed (70 per cent above the national average), while Oregon residents have yielded only $940 in premiums per 1,000 mail pieces.

This model gave United a sense of direction with its *lead-generation process, but it needed to be further refined. For example, this model did not evaluate the relative value of each consumer characteristic (would North Carolina consultants generate greater premiums per 1,000 mail pieces than Oregon gas station owners?).

So United developed a second lead-generation model to study the relative importance of various consumer traits. A weighted score value was assigned to each lead characteristic that could be associated with the premiums generated. Then, the "perfect prospect" was assigned a value of 1,000; a worthless prospect was scored a zero.

Here are the score values assigned to selected occupational groups: auto sales and leasing, 0; food stores, 28; restaurants, 57; gas stations, 107; graphics services, 120; and home-care services, 178. Here are the score values assigned to selected non-occupational categories (note: a business may fall into two or more categories): individual ownership, 28; business owner known by name, 50; use of a post office box, 51; and prior response made to United Group, 90.

Each record (business) in United's master file has been scored by adding the value of various occupational and nonoccupational characteristics. The greater the score value, the better the prospect. This second model was tested via more than 300,000 mailings in which leads were placed into 13 groups based upon their total score value.

In this test, accounts with higher scores had a better quantity of leads for salespeople to call on – as well as better levels of premiums. For example, businesses with score values of 350 or more accounted for 21 per cent of United Group's data base and represented 27 per cent of its leads and 26 per cent of its sales. Businesses scoring 225 or higher accounted for 91 per cent of United's data base, and represented 92 per cent of its leads and 97 per cent of its total sales.

After seeing the results of this test, United decided to restrict future mailings to accounts with a minimum 225 total score. The firm estimates that it will save more than $238,000 in annual mailing costs through use of this model.

In the future, United plans to use two separate models: one for mail and one for telemarketing.

'Marketing', Evans, J.R. and Berman, B., (4th edn, Macmillan, 1990)

Text organisation

1. Below are four summaries of the text. Decide which one you think most fully and accurately expresses the main ideas of the text.

   (a) United Group, which sells hospital insurance policies, largely to self-employed business people, developed a system for making its marketing more effective. This system was based on the responsiveness of potential customers which was measured by how many sales were made by the sales agents, the value of the insurance policies taken out, the number of policies which were not renewed and the size of the claims made on policies. On the basis of this information, a mathematical model was developed which showed United which groups of occupations were their best customers. Thus they found that gas station owners were very profitable for them, while consultants bought far less of their insurance. The mathematical model also gave United information about which areas produced the best sales results. North Carolina, for example, proved to be a much better area to sell their insurance policies in than Oregon.

   (b) United Group sells hospital-stay insurance policies to small businesses. These include such types of business as repair people, printers, electricians and restaurant owners. The company sells its policies through more than 1,000 agents who must have 750,000 sales leads each year in order to remain fully occupied. To get these 750,000 leads, United have to send out 15 million mailings and make over 10 million phone calls. Using a mathematical model to discover which groups were its best customers, United discovered that gas station owners were most profitable. Thus the amount of premiums which they provided, $1,446 per 1,000 mailings, was 18 per cent above the average for all occupations. After having made a second model which gave scores to different customer characteristics (e.g. 28 for food stores, 107 for gas stations), it was found that businesses with score values of 350 or more accounted for 21 per cent of United Group's potential customers. They also represented 27 of its leads and 26 per cent of its sales.

   (c) United Group sells hospital insurance plans, mainly to self-employed business people. It sells its products through about 1,000 sales agents who follow up sales leads obtained by United Group by means of mail shots and telephone calls. The firm has done a sophisticated mathematical analysis of the results of these methods to see which groups provide the best customers. The company found that certain occupational groups (e.g. gas station owners) and certain areas (e.g. North Carolina) are most profitable for it. To gain more information about who were the best potential customers, United created a second model based on giving different values to various consumer characteristics. By adding these characteristic scores together, it discovered which businesses provided the most leads and the highest percentage of sales. This information will influence United's mailing policy in future and should save it more than a quarter of a million dollars on postage costs.

   (d) United Group, a hospital insurance group in America, sells its policies only to self-employed business people. United sells its products through agents who also market other insurance companies' policies. United uses various methods of marketing, including mail pieces and telephone calls. To judge the effectiveness of its marketing, United worked out a mathematical model based on responses to its mailings and phone calls. This model showed that it was only worth dealing with certain types of occupations (e.g. gas station owners) and certain areas of America (e.g. North Carolina). A second model which United developed gave weighted values to a few characteristics of customers which United thought were important. This model showed that customers who scored 350 or more produced 97% of United's total sales. Therefore in future United will only send mailings to those companies. This will give United a one-off saving of $238,000.

2. This exercise gives you further practice in understanding the use of pronouns and other referring phrases. Find the pronouns or phrases which refer to the following parts of the text. The first one is done for you.
   (i) 'United Group' in line 1 is referred to by 'Its' in line 2.
   (ii) 'self-employed repair people, printers, electricians and restaurant owners' in lines 2–3 are referred to by _________ in line _________ .
   (iii) '750,000 qualified sales leads' in line 7 are referred to by _________ in line _________ .
   (iv) From 'the lists of small businesses ...' (line 9) to '... and *Dun & Bradstreet New Business*' (line 10) is referred to by _________ in line _________
   (v) 'the *Yellow Pages* and *Dun & Bradstreet New Business*' in line 10 are referred to by _________ in line _________ .
   (vi) 'United Group' (line 16) is referred to by _________ in line _________ .
   (vii) 'consultants' in line 20 are referred to by _________ in line _________ .
   (viii) From 'Among occupational groups ...' (line 18) to '... per 1,000 mail pieces' (line 26) is referred to by _________ in line _________ .
   (ix) From 'So United developed.' (line 32) to 'the better the prospect' (line 45) is referred to by _________ in line _________ .
   (x) From 'This second model ...' (line 45) to... 'total score value' (line 47) is referred to by _________ in line _________ and by _________ in line _________ .
   (xi) 'Leads' in line 46 are referred to by _________ in line _________ .
   (xii) From 'United decided ...' (line 54) to '... 225 total score' (line 55) is referred to by _________ in line _________ .
   (xiii) 'The firm' (line 55) is referred to by _________ in line _________ .

Comprehension

3. Decide whether the following statements are true or false according to the text. Identify the lines where you find your answers.

	Statement	True/false	Line numbers
(i)	United mainly sells insurance to small business people who employ one or two workers.		
(ii)	United's sales agents only sell the insurance products of one company.		
(iii)	United's sales agents will, if necessary, visit a customer several times to sell a policy.		
(iv)	Each United agent visits about 1,000 potential customers a year.		
(v)	It takes a total of 33 mailings and phone calls to produce one United sales lead.		

4. Below are some figures taken from the text. Match each figure to the description underneath which refers to it.

(i)	$1,446	(iii)	1,000	(v)	$2,080	(vii)	$940
(ii)	18%	(iv)	$554	(vi)	70%		

(a) The figure above average country-wide premium sales for people living in one US state
(b) The amount of premiums bought by garage owners for a given number of mailings
(c) The average sale of premiums in Oregon for a given number of mailings
(d) The amount of premiums bought by North Carolina residents for a given number of mailings
(e) The number of mailings used to calculate the average sale of premiums
(f) The amount of premiums bought by consultants from a given number of mailings
(g) The percentage by which average premium sales to gas station owners exceed average premium sales to other job categories

5. (a) Which item of information from those listed below did the first mathematical model *not* give?
   (i) Average sale of premiums to consultants for a given amount of mail pieces
   (ii) Whether occupation or location had more effect on average premium sales
   (iii) Whether consultants or garage owners in a particular location were better customers
   (iv) Whether one area of the country produced more premium sales from a mailing than another

(b) How did United change their mathematical model to obtain this missing information?
(c) In the second mathematical model, what score would the best potential customer get? What score would the worst potential customer get?

6. In the second mathematical model, what would be the score values for the following categories?

Category	Score value
(i) A home-care service which had contacted United before the current mailing	
(ii) A restaurant whose owners' names were available	
(iii) A small supermarket owned by one person	
(iv) A company making illustrations for magazines which received mail through a post office box	

7. Put the actions below into their correct order according to the text.

Action	Order
(i) The second model was checked to see what results it would give.	
(ii) Businesses which United had on record were given a total score based on different individual factors.	
(iii) Based on their total score, businesses were divided into a number of different groups.	
(iv) It was assumed that businesses with higher total scores were more likely to become customers.	

8. Fill in the missing information for the pie charts below, using lines 72–81 of the text.

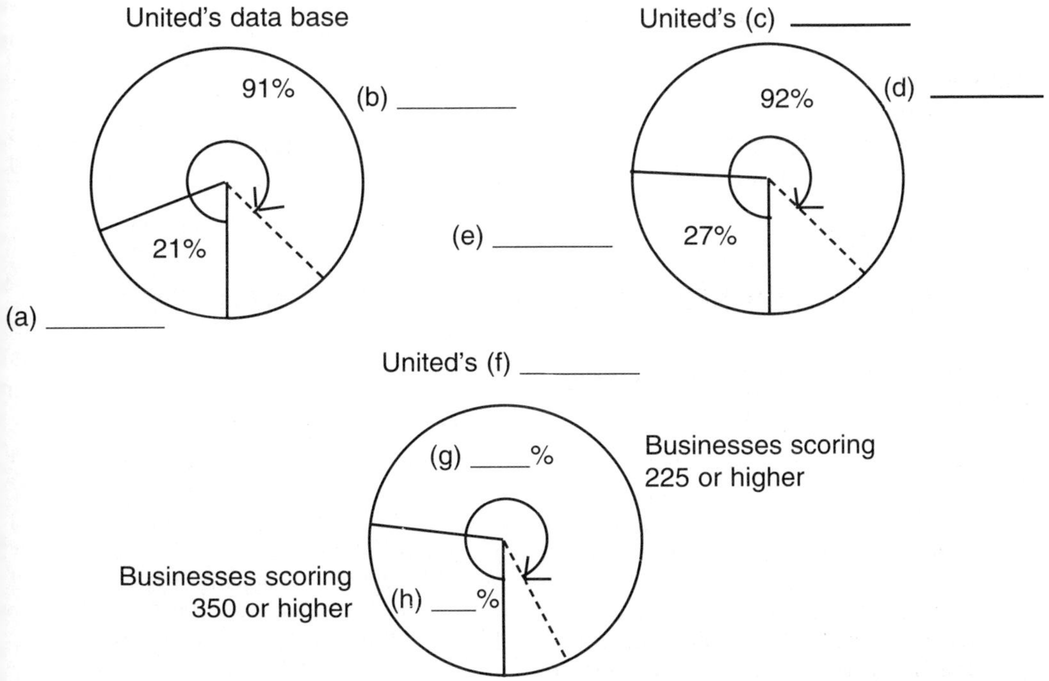

9. (a) What decision did United Group take on the basis of its results from using the second model?
   (b) What result does United think this decision will have for it?

Vocabulary

10. Here is a summary of the text with some words missing. Complete the summary, using one word from the text for each gap. Make sure you use a different word for each gap and that you put it in the correct grammatical form.

United Group, a hospital insurance company, uses sales agents who (i) ______ sell its policies. (ii) ______ for those agents are (iii) ______ by means of mailings and telephone calls. In relation to these methods, United wanted to find out which groups were most (iv) ______ and profitable. These two aspects could be judged on (v) ______ like the number of sales made, the amount of business placed and (vi) ______ in insurance policies previously taken out. A mathematical model based on such information showed which occupations and geographical areas (vii) ______ most premiums. To gain more information the model was (viii) ______ so that it (ix) ______ the importance of a number of additional consumer factors. Each of these consumer (x) ______ was (xi) ______ a value which, added together, showed the potential worth of a lead. Because potential customers with total scores of 225 or above (xii) ______ for 92% of leads and 97% of sales, United decided to (xiii) ______ future mailings to this group.

Text 10.2 US banks stake out insurance battlefield

Skim and scan

(a) What are ‘annuities’?
(b) Does the Office of the Comptroller of the Currency in the United States think that annuities are banking or insurance products?

US banks stake out insurance battlefield

THE TINY outpost of Banks, Oregon (population 489), is an unlikely battleground for the struggle between US banks and insurers over whether banks should be allowed into the insurance business. Yet this small town, wedged between the city of Portland and the Pacific Ocean, has been the setting for one of a series of convoluted legal actions which will ultimately determine whether banks can use their networks to sell insurance products around the country.

This Oregon town is home to one of the first nationwide insurance marketing efforts by a bank, the Portland-based US National Bank. Taking advantage of a legislative loophole which allows nationally chartered banks (as opposed to those organised under state laws) to sell insurance from towns with populations of less than 5,000, US National markets insurance products by direct mail throughout the US. Similar operations have sprung up in small towns all over the country as banks seek to expand the range of products they sell to their customers.

A flurry of legal actions over such operations, brought by insurance agents eager to protect business, is currently winding its way through the federal court system. The right of US National to continue its operations in Banks was upheld in July by a federal appeals court in Washington. But the latest ruling of its kind, handed down by the federal appeals court in Houston, was a setback for the banking industry. This judgment, delivered against NationsBank, the North Carolina-based bank, could severely restrict the ability of banks to sell annuities, a business with bank sales put at $15bn a year.

According to the Houston ruling, annuities – contracts which pay a set amount periodically to an investor for life in return for a single lump-sum payment – are a type of insurance contract, and so should be subject to the same rules as other insurance products. That runs counter to a ruling earlier this year by the Office of the Comptroller of the Currency, the arm of the US Treasury charged with regulating nationally chartered banks. The OCC concluded that annuities were banking rather than insurance products, a view it continued to adhere to yesterday.

For banks which have grown accustomed to picking their way through the discrepancies between banking and insurance regulation and between federal and state legislation, such conflicts are nothing new. "We've been in litigation for three years," says Mr Tom Brumley, president of the small, Kentucky-based Owensboro National Bank, which has assets of just $370m. Mr Brumley has been fighting the Kentucky insurance regulators over whether the bank can sell insurance products at all in the state. Echoing the ambitions of bankers around the country, he says he wants to use his existing network to sell more products to the 22,000 households which comprise the bank's customer base.

Kentucky law forbids bank employees 6
from selling insurance. The question now, to be decided in the federal appeals court in Cincinnati, is whether such state legislation has primacy over federal law, or whether Mr Brumley's bank can enter the insurance business.

Complicating the picture for the banks 7
has been a lack of clarity in some of the rulings so far. The Washington judgment found that banks could sell insurance from small towns – apparently leaving it open to banks with insurance operations headquarters in such places to use any method to sell insurance anywhere in the US, including through their existing bank branch network. Last week's ruling in Houston, though, appeared to limit banks to selling insurance only in small towns.

Bankers hope that such discrepancies 8
will eventually be ironed out in the *supreme court. Given the vested interest involved, most hold out little hope that Congress will attempt to clarify the issue with new legislation, a route recommended by the Washington court.

'Financial Times' 1 September 1993

Comprehension

1. Say whether the following statements about Banks, Oregon are true or false according to the text. Show where in the text you find your answers.

	Statement	True/false	Line numbers
(i)	There is no legal problem about whether a bank can market nationally its insurance products from Banks.		
(ii)	US National Bank chose to market its insurance products from Banks because of that town's size.		
(iii)	If US National Bank had been controlled by state laws it couldn't have marketed insurance products from Banks, Oregon.		
(iv)	Banks, Oregon is the only small town in the USA from which banks are trying to market insurance products.		

2. Say whether the following decisions *supported* or *opposed* banks selling insurance.
   (i) The federal appeals court decision in July in Washington
   (ii) The federal appeals court decision in Houston
   (iii) The earlier decision by the Office of the Comptroller of the Currency
   (iv) The most recent decision by the Office of the Comptroller of the Currency

3. Match the institution on the left with the decision which it made.

	Institution		Decision
(i)	Federal appeals court in Washington	(a)	Ruled that annuities are an insurance product
(ii)	Federal appeals court in Houston	(b)	Ruled that annuities are a banking product
(iii)	Office of the Comptroller of the Currency	(c)	Ruled that US banks could sell insurance

4. (a) Are conflicts between banking and insurance rules in America unusual?
   (b) What other type of legal conflict can occur in America, according to the text?
   (c) What sentence in the text gives you the answers to these two questions?

5. Choose the correct alternatives in the following paragraph so that it is correct according to the text.

   The Owenboro National Bank has been in conflict with Kentucky (banking/insurance) regulations about whether it can sell insurance products (nationally/in Kentucky). Tom Brumley, the president, (wants to develop/has) a client base to whom his bank can sell insurance. (National/Kentucky) law prevents staff of banks selling insurance, although (Kentucky/national) law allows it. The question of which law has priority will be decided by a (state/federal) appeals court.

6. (a) Did the federal appeals court in Washington say that banks could sell insurance *in* or *from* small towns?
   (b) Did the federal appeals court in Houston say that banks could sell insurance *in* or *from* small towns?
   (c) Which decision would be better for banks wanting to sell insurance?

7. (a) Will the problems connected with banks selling insurance be decided by the courts or by the US Congress, according to the text?
   (b) What is the reason for your answer to 7(a)?

Vocabulary

8. Find words or phrases in the text which have the meanings below. The line numbers indicate in what part of the text you will find the required word or phrase.

Meaning	Word in text
Lines 0–39 (i) situated (ii) complicated (iii) unclear part of a law (iv) large number of something in a short period (v) negative result	
Lines 40–72 (vi) contradicts (vii) section (viii) hold (ix) differences (x) legal conflict (xi) agreeing with	
Lines 73–103 (xii) form (xiii) authority over (xiv) removed (xv) group which gains from some situation	

Text organisation

9. Form nine complete sentences by combining sentence parts from (a), (b) and (c). Each sentence needs a part from (a), from (b) and from (c). Then re-order these complete sentences so that they form an accurate summary of the text. Write out your final version in full before checking the answer in the key.
   (a) (i) A federal court in Washigngton originally
       (ii) Here the dispute is over whether Kentucky state law
       (iii) A small town in America, Banks, Oregon,
       (iv) It seems likely that the whole question
       (v) In this case it was ruled that annuities
       (vi) American law apparently permits

(vii) The problem is further complicated in that it is not clear
(viii) Insurance agents, wanting to protect their own business,
(ix) Such legal disputes are not new, however, as is

(b) (i) is at the centre of legal battles about whether
(ii) shown by the situation of a Kentucky bank which
(iii) will have to be decided in the American Supreme Court
(iv) supported the bank's position, but a recent
(v) which forbids banks selling insruance
(vi) if banks can only sell insurance in towns with
(vii) nationally regulated banks to market insurance
(viii) have taken legal actions against banks
(ix) were an insurance product and not

(c) (i) which have tried to use this law.
(ii) has priority over federal law, which allows it.
(iii) rather than by new legislation.
(iv) banks should be allowed to sell insurance.
(v) legal decision could change this situation.
(vi) less than 5,000 people or also from them.
(vii) from towns with populations under 5,000.
(viii) a banking one as the US Treasury claims.
(ix) has been trying to sell insurance products for three years.

Answer key

Unit 1 The basis of insurance

Text 1.1

Skim and scan

(a) Informal
(b) A textbook

Text organisation

1. (ii) Paragraph 5
 (iii) Paragraph 4
 (iv) Paragraph 2
 (v) Paragraph 6
 (vi) Paragraph 1

Comprehension

2. (i) $0
 (ii) $0
 (iii) $100,000
 (iv) $100,000
 (v) $800
 (vi) $100,000
 (vii) $800
 (viii) $100,000

3. (i) False. Insurance does not stop them from happening but can predict them (paragraph 1).
 (ii) True (paragraph 1).
 (iii) False. A few people suffer losses but everyone in the system has to pay for them (paragraph 3).
 (iv) False. He/she gets peace of mind even when nothing bad happens to him/her (paragraph 6).

4. The premium is the sum of money which each individual in an insurance scheme pays into the pool. As a result of paying this, the individual protects himself against exposure to loss and he receives compensation if he does have a loss. In this way there is a redistribution of an individual's loss among all the scheme's members.

5. (a) (i) 33 is the number of homes it is estimated will burn down in one year.
 (ii) 5,000 is the number of homeowners in the insurance scheme described in the text.
 (b) Because it is estimated that it costs $100,000 to replace each house and there are 5,000 house owners in this insurance scheme. It is also estimated that 33 houses out of the 5,000 will burn down. The loss per year will, therefore, be 33 x $100,000 = $330,000. In order for 5,000 houseowners to supply this amount in the insurance pool, each houseowner must pay $\frac{\$330,000}{\$5,000}$ = $660.
 Each householder was, in fact, charged $800 by the company running the insurance scheme. The extra $140 was to pay the company's administration costs and to give it some profit.

Vocabulary

6. (a) (iii) (b) (ii) (c) (i) (d) (iv) (e) (ii)

Text 1.2

Skim and scan

(i) Heading B
(ii) Heading A
(iii) Heading C

Text organisation

1. (ii) 'The law' (line 3)
   (iii) 'The law' (line 3)
   (iv) 'a contract' (line 5)
   (v) 'his or her own life' (line 9)
   (vi) 'property' (line 11)
   (vii) 'property' (line 19)
   (viii) 'Contracts of insurance' (line 28)
   (ix) 'anyone (who) applies for insurance' (line 30)
   (x) 'if he has recently had a heart attack' (line 34)
   (xi) 'This' in line 41 refers to the whole previous sentence.

Comprehension

2.

Insurable interest	Indemnity	Utmost good faith
(iv) (lines 10–13) (vi) (lines 13–15)	(ii) (lines 16–19) (v) (lines 21–23)	(i) (lines 30–33) (iii) (lines 39–41)

3. (a) x (b) ✓ (c) x (d) x (e) ✓

Vocabulary

4. (i) effected: produced ('effect' as a verb, i.e. 'effect[2]')
   (ii) liabilities: the amount of debt which must be paid (definition 3)
   (iii) indemnity: a promise to pay for the replacement or repair of loss or damage ('indemnity' as noun)
   (iv) to grant: to give (definition 2)
   (v) proposer: a person intending to take out insurance (notice here that the definition of this meaning of 'proposer' is in the explanation of 'proposal')
   (vi) prone: likely to suffer (from something undesirable) (definition 1)

5. (a) (iii)
   (b) (ii)
   (c) (i)
   (d) (ii)
   (e) (iv)

6.

Nouns	**Adjectives**
insurance insured insurer	insured insurable insurance

Unit 2 Life and health insurance

Text 2.1

Skim and scan

(a) Utmost good faith is not discussed.
(b) There is no limit to a person's insurable interest in him/herself. (lines 29–30)

Text organisation

1. (i) 4
   (ii) 2
   (iii) 5
   (iv) 1
   (v) 3
   (vi) 7
   (vii) 6

Comprehension

2. (a) (ii) (lines 1–5)
   (b) (iv) (lines 6–8)
   (c) (i) (lines 20–24)
   (d) (iv) (lines 29–33)

3. The key point is that the person or organisation taking out life insurance on a particular person must have an insurable interest in that person at the time when the insurance policy is taken out (lines 36–37).

4. (i) ✓
   (ii) x
   (iii) x
   (iv) ✓
   (v) x
   (vi) ✓

Vocabulary

5. (i) (f)
   (ii) (a)
   (iii) (i)
   (iv) (d)
   (v) (l)
   (vi) (b)
   (vii) (j)
   (viii) (e)
   (ix) (g)
   (x) (k)
   (xi) (h)
   (xii) (c)

Text 2.2

Skim and scan

(a) 'Outstrip' means to rise more quickly than something else. In this case it means that the cost of health insurance is rising more quickly than inflation in general.

(b) (i) BUPA is 'the largest private health group' (lines 16–17).
    (ii) Laing and Buisson are a 'health care analyst' (lines 77–78).

Vocabulary

1. (i) subscribers (line 5)
   (ii) steep (line 9)
   (iii) scales (line 19)
   (iv) impose (line 24)
   (v) absorbed (line 30)
   (vi) freezing (line 33)
   (vii) reflected (line 44)
   (viii) sharply (line 49)
   (ix) smooth (line 52)
   (x) restrictions (line 58)
   (xi) retaining (line 63)
   (xii) resilient (line 74)
   (xiii) peak (line 82)

Comprehension

2 (i) The amount by which the cost of private medical insurance increased on the day the article was published (lines 1–4).
  (ii) In lines 6–8, 18 per cent refers to how much more some elderly people will have to pay for their private medical insurance. In lines 77–87, 18 per cent is the percentage of the total population who will be members of private medical insurance schemes.
  (ii) The amount by which BUPA is increasing premiums on its medical insurance policies for older people who have more protection (lines 16–19).
  (iv) The amount by which medical insurance premiums may be reduced for some younger people who have limited protection (lines 20–21)
  (v) The average cost of a claim made by a patient under 60 last year (lines 41–42)
  (vi) The average cost of a claim made by a patient over 60 last year (lines 43–45)
  (vii) 15–20 per cent is the amount by which BUPA can reduce medical insurance premiums for those people who agree to some limitations on how they are treated if they become ill (lines 56–65).
  15–20 per cent is the annual increase in the cost of medical care (lines 66–71).
  (viii) The reduction in the last three years of the number of people covered by private medical insurance (lines 78–80)
  (ix) The number of people who had private medical insurance in the year before the article was written (lines 81–82)
  (x) The maximum number of people who had private medical insurance (in 1990) (lines 82–83)

3.

(i)	Some young people will get a premium reduction. (lines 20–21)	Older people will pay premiums between 10 and 18.2% higher. (lines 16–19)
(ii)	Young people use medical services less. (lines 38–45)	Older people use medical services more. (lines 41–45)
(iii)	Less for some young people. (lines 20–21)	Generally higher for the old. (lines 16–19)
(iv)	Younger people: £983 (lines 41–42)	Older people: £1,390 (lines 43–45)

4. (i) False (lines 11–12)
   (ii) True (lines 22–26)
   (iii) False (lines 41–45)
   (iv) False (lines 51–55)
   (v) True (lines 56–65)
   (vi) False (lines 66–71)
   (vii) True (lines 72–76)

5. (a) 18% (lines 85–87)
   It will be an increase of 7% because the percentage covered by private medical insurance now is 11%. (lines 83–84)

Text organisation

6. (ii) however (or nevertheless)
   (iii) if
   (iv) as a result
   (v) nevertheless (or however)
   (vi) in order
   (vii) for example
   (viii) at the same time
   (ix) despite/in spite of the fact that

Unit 3 Pensions and pension funds

Text 3.1

Skim and scan

(a) There are two. (line 10)
(b) One is called a 'defined-benefit plan' (lines 10–11). The other is called a 'defined-contribution plan' (line 14).

Text organisation

1. (i) Paragraph 5
   (ii) Paragraph 1
   (iii) Paragraph 7
   (iv) Paragraph 2
   (v) Paragraph 4
   (vi) Paragraph 3
   (vii) Paragraph 6

Comprehension

2. (a) 90% (lines 5–6)
   (b) 'Most of the others' (lines 6–7)
   (c) 'Half' (lines 7–9)

3. (a) The size of the pension is decided first (lines 10–13).
   (b) The amounts that a person will pay for his/her pension is decided first (lines 13–17).

4. (i) x
   (ii) ✓
   (iii) ✓
   (iv) x
   (v) ✓
   (vi) ✓
   (vii) x
   (viii) x
   (ix) x
   (x) ✓

5. (i) (b) government
   (ii) (d) employer
   (iii) (a) labour and management
   (iv) (c) employee

6. (i) 3
   (ii) 1
   (iii) 5
   (iv) 2
   (v) 4

7. (a) The number of old people in America is rising (lines 42–44).
   (b) The rise in the number of old people has greatly increased the economic influence of pension funds (lines 42–44). This means that pension funds play a very important part in financial markets in the USA (lines 45–46).

Vocabulary

8. (b) (i) disposition
   (ii) defined-contribution plan
   (iii) provisions
   (iv) With respect to
   (v) defined-distribution plan
   (vi) entity
   (vii) formula
   (viii) eligible
   (ix) collective-bargaining process
   (x) projected
   (xi) accumulates

Text 3.2

Skim and scan

(a) Europe ('the Continent', line 6)
(b) 'Defined-benefit' schemes (lines 32–34)

Vocabulary

1. (i) cater for
   (ii) bodies
   (iii) instrument
   (iv) onerous
   (v) constituted
   (vi) exemptions
   (vii) come back into the limelight
   (viii) governed
   (ix) in conjunction with
   (x) abrogate

Comprehension

2. (a) Yes (lines 1–3)
   (b) The disadvantages of such a system are, first, that it would depend on a company making consistent profits and, second, that it would not give much security (lines 3–6). No advantages of such a system are mentioned.

3. (a) The three sources of income are:
   (i) Contributions of employees (lines 11–12)
   (ii) Contributions of employers (lines 12–13)
   (iii) Income from previously acquired investments (lines 13–14)
   (b) Their investment activities are tax-exempt (lines 8–9).

4. (i) False (lines 15–18)
   (ii) False (lines 19–21)
   (iii) True (lines 22–24)
   (iv) True (lines 24–27)
   (v) False (lines 28–31)

5. <u>Most</u> pension schemes today are of the <u>'defined-benefit'</u> type. With this type of scheme the pension depends on the <u>final salary</u> of the employee. Such pensions <u>take</u> account of increases in inflation. <u>Defined-contribution</u> schemes, on the other hand, are becoming more popular now that inflation has decreased. The investment policies required by both types of pension are <u>different</u>.

Text organisation

6. (i) 12 (ii) 10 (iii) 11

Unit 4 Property insurance

Text 4.1

Skim and scan

(i) Heading E
(ii) Heading C
(iii) Heading A
(iv) Heading B
(v) Heading D

Text organisation

1. (i) '(the people who work at) Royal Insurance' (line 1)
   (ii) 'that we, as one of Britain's leading household insurance companies, should recognise such care by using the fairest, most accurate premium assessment system available today' (lines 6–10)
   (iii) the person reading the leaflet
   (iv) 'householders' (line 14)
   (v) 'your home' (line 27)
   (vi) 'one million householders' (line 32)
   (vii) 'the coupon' (line 43)
   (viii) Royal Insurance (not in text, but understood)
   (ix) 'new for old cover' (lines 52–53)
   (x) 'items claimed for' (lines 54–55)

Comprehension

2. (a) They want to attract 'careful householders' (line 2).
   (b) They use 'the fairest, most accurate premium assessment system available today' (lines 8–10).
   (c) 'the premium could be less than that charged by their present insurer' (lines 14–16).

3. First, your claim will be 'dealt with promptly' (lines 19–20) and, second, you will not have 'unnecessary argument' (lines 21–22).

4. (a) 150 years (lines 28–29)
   (b) one million (lines 32–34)

5. For these answers you need not use exactly the same words as used here but the meaning of your answer must be the same.
   (i) Royal Insurance will ensure that you know exactly what your insurance covers you for if you take out a household insurance policy with them.
   (ii) You will be eligible to take out a household insurance policy with Royal Insurance if you can tick 'yes' to the six questions in the application form.
   (iii) If you return the coupon or phone them, Royal Insurance will send you a free quotation by return of post.
   (iv) Royal Insurance give 'new for old cover' when you make a claim for lost or damaged articles.
   (v) Other insurance companies will only pay you the original cost of an item when you make a claim for lost or damaged articles.

6. (i) No
   (ii) Yes (lines 59–60)
   (iii) No
   (iv) Yes (lines 65–68)

7. (a) Would not qualify – the house is used as a hairdresser's so breaks qualification number 5.
   (b) Would qualify.
   (c) Would not qualify – the house is older than 1871 so breaks qualification number 6.

Vocabulary

8.

(i)	(c)	(vi)	(i)
(ii)	(h)	(vii)	(e)
(iii)	(a)	(viii)	(g)
(iv)	(f)	(ix)	(b)
(v)	(d)		

9. (i) qualify
   (ii) bungalow
   (iii) semi-detached
   (iv) terraced
   (v) widowed
   (vi) spouse
   (vii) expire
   (viii) prerequisite
   (ix) occupied
   (x) 5 lever mortice locks
   (xi) neighbourhood/home watch

Text 4.2

Skim and scan

(a) 'Shop around' here means to ask how much different insurance companies are charging for insurance in order to find the policy which is the best value.

(b) 'Telesure' are 'telephone-biased insurance brokers' (lines 5–6). 'Direct Line' and 'Guardian Direct' are both direct insurers (lines 49–50 and 77–78).

Text organisation

1. (a) (i) From 'Research by Telesure ...' to '... 30 or 40 per cent in many.' (lines 5–9)
   (ii) 'Insurers' (line 14)
   (iii) 'claims' (line 15)
   (iv) 'loyal (or lazy) customers' (lines 28–29)
   (v) From 'if their premiums . . .' to '... in the same way' (lines 30–33)
   (vi) 'Direct Line' (line 49)
   (vii) 'a price war' (line 56)
   (viii) 'things' (line 69)
   (ix) 'trying to compete on other factors, such as service' (lines 73–74)
   (x) From 'for consumers... .' to '... for low prices' (lines 79–81)

   (b) (i) 'they' (line 73)
   (ii) 'both' (line 87)
   (iii) 'those' (line 89), 'their' (line 90), 'They' (line 91) and 'them' (line 94)
   (iv) 'Some of them' (line 98) and 'others' (line 99)

Comprehension

2. (i) False ('You might find a quote for half your present premium . . .', lines 2–3)
   (ii) True (lines 7–9)
   (iii) False ('in many [cases], line 11)

3. (i) x
   (ii) ✓ (lines 15–17)
   (iii) ✓ (lines 21–24)
   (iv) x
   (v) ✓ (lines 37–40)

4. (a) 20% represents the amount by which car insurance premiums have been increasing annually over the last few years.

   (b) This figure, according to the text, is due to the fact that car crime (e.g. car theft) and the recent economic recession cost the insurance companies so much money that they had to increase their premiums by this amount each year (lines 35–37).

   (c) Although the text doesn't state it directly, the recession might have led to the premium increase because there were more false claims. That is, because people had less money, they might have tried to get some money from the insurance companies by false claims. (Can you think of any other ways in which the recession could have caused the insurance companies to increase premiums?)

5. (a) (iii) (lines 47–53)
   (b) (ii) (lines 56–61)
   (c) (i) (lines 62–65)

6. (a) They could compete on service (lines 72–74).
   (b) The example given is that companies could offer 'smoother claims procedures' (line 75).
   (c) He doesn't think it's as good as price competition. Thus he says it's 'far less easy for consumers to shop around for good service than for low prices' (lines 79–81).

7. (i) TB (lines 97–98)
   (ii) DI (lines 89–90)
   (iii) DI (lines 91–92)
   (iv) TB (lines 99–100)
   (v) TB (lines 98–99)
   (vi) DI (lines 98–100)
   (vii) DI and TB (lines 89–90 and 97–98)

Vocabulary

8. (i) random (line 11)
   (ii) model (line 17)
   (iii) renewal (line 21)
   (iv) let alone (line 26)
   (v) compunction (line 36)
   (vi) bumping up (line 36)
   (vii) to feel tied (line 42)
   (viii) imitators (line 51)
   (ix) murmuring (line 55)
   (x) entrant (line 77)

Unit 5 Credit insurance

Text 5.1

Skim and scan

(a) 'Cover' means protection by insurance.
(b) 'Multi-market insurance' applies to the UK and most OECD markets (lines 28–30).

Text organisation

1. (i) Heading C
   (ii) Heading G
   (iii) Heading E
   (iv) Heading A
   (v) Heading D
   (vi) Heading B
   (vii) Heading F

Vocabulary

2. (i) risk analysts
   (ii) get rid of
   (iii) are added together
   (iv) decided beforehand
   (v) expected
   (vi) having gone out of business
   (vii) lasting a long time
   (viii) failure to pay
   (ix) extremely
   (x) thought sure to pay
   (xi) always
   (xii) before
   (xiii) resulting
   (xiv) occur

Comprehension

3. (i) 75%–100% (line 44)
   (ii) up to 100% (line 50)
   (iii) 80%–85% (line 17)
   (iv) 100% (above agreed amount of loss) (lines 10–11)
   (v) 90% (lines 31–32)
   (vi) 70%–90% (line 40)

4. (a) (a) (iv) 'first loss'
   (b) (i) annual aggregate
   (c) (iii) 100% cover
   (d) (ii) maximum liability
   (b) (i) The company seeking insurance will pay this (lines 5–6).
   (ii) The company seeking insurance will pay this (lines 7–9).
   (iii) The insurance company will pay this (lines 10–11).

5. Whole turnover: (b) (c) (f) (h)
   Pre-delivery risk: (d) (i)
   Multi-market: (a) (e) (f) (g)

6. (iii) (lines 34–37)

7. (a) Datum Line cover (line 41)
   (b) (i) It provides cover if large customers do not pay because they go bankrupt. (lines 38–39)
   (ii) Financial advice can be provided. (lines 39–40)
   (iii) The amount it insures varies between 70–90% (line 40).

8. (i) True (lines 44–45)
   (ii) False. It can also insure against a single company making more than one purchase (line 42).
   (iii) False (lines 42–44)
   (iv) False (line 50)
   (v) True (lines 46–48)
   (vi) True (lines 48–50)

Text 5.2

Skim and scan

(a) It means there are five different export insurance premiums in the new German system.
(b) 'Hermes' is the name of the German system of export insurance.

Text organisation

1. (i) Paragraph 6
   (ii) Paragraph 3
   (iii) Paragraph 9
   (iv) Paragraph 2
   (v) Paragraph 7
   (vi) Paragraph 1
   (vii) Paragraph 5
   (viii) Paragraph 4
   (ix) Paragraph 8

Comprehension

2. (a) 50 years (line 1–4)
   (b) (i) 66% (lines 4–7)
   (ii) 100% (lines 7–9)

3. (a) They criticise the fact that insurance premiums to the East Germans' former communist trading partners have been increased (lines 18–22).
   (b) It is implied that they seem to benefit because they do not export as much to ex-communist countries as East Germany did (lines 18–23).
   (c) The German government hopes to reduce the amount of money they had to spend on the previous export insurance system (lines 34–39).

4. (a) It requires that export credit insurance schemes are independent and self-supporting (lines 28–33).
   (b) No, it wasn't (lines 31–33).

5. (i) 4.5 billion Deutschmarks
   (ii) 5.1 billion Deutschmarks
   (iii) 7.5 billion Deutschmarks

6. (i) (f) (lines 49–53), (d) (lines 4–9 and 49–53)
   (ii) (c) (lines 64–68)
   (iii (a) (lines 56–61), (e) (lines 56–61)
   (iv) (b) (lines 61–63)
   (v) (b) (lines 61–63)
   (vi) (a) (lines 58–61)

7. (i) False (lines 49–53)
   (ii) True (lines 70–72)
   (iii) True (lines 72–76)
   (iv) False (lines 76–78)
   (v) False (lines 80–83)

Vocabulary

8. (ii) I slow payers
   (iii) I unhappy
   (iv) I uncompromising
   (v) I for a sum equal to
   (vi) F quick rise
   (vii) I set aside
   (viii) F unpaid
   (ix) I considered most creditworthy
   (x) I are not utilised
   (xi) I avoided
   (xii) I totally disregarded
   (xiii) F in support of
   (xiv) F clearly

Text organisation

9. (i) 4
   (ii) 2
   (iii) 1
   (iv) 3

Unit 6 Insurance policies

Text 6.1

Skim and scan

(a) Building and contents insurance
(b) Heading A – (iv) Loss or damage
Heading B – (ii) Additional cover

Text organisation

1. (ii) the buildings which are being insured by this policy (these are not directly mentioned in the text but they are understood)
   (iii) 'floor slabs' (line 35)
   (iv) the holder of this policy (this is understood from the context)
   (v) the same cause that led to 'loss of or ... damage to outdoor swimming pools, gates or fences' (lines 38–41)
   (vi) when there was 'loss of or damage to outdoor swimming pools, gates or fences' (lines 38–41)
   (vii) the place where the insured building is located (not directly stated in the text, but understood)
   (viii) this whole part of the text labelled 'Section 1' (i.e. lines 1–97)
   (ix) 'any government or local authority requirement' (lines 71–72)
   (x) 'your new dwelling' (line 90)

Comprehension

2. (i) ✓ (paragraph 9)
   (ii) ✓ (paragraph 3)
   (iii) x
   (iv) x

3. (i) will <u>not</u> be paid for (line 4)
   (ii) will <u>not</u> be paid for (line 9)
   (iii) <u>will</u> be paid for (line 11)
   (iv) <u>will</u> be paid for (line 11)
   (v) will <u>not</u> be paid for (line 17)
   (vi) <u>will</u> be paid for (line 22)
   (vii) will <u>not</u> be paid for (lines 23–24)
   (viii) will <u>not</u> be paid for (lines 33–34)
   (ix) will <u>not</u> be paid for (lines 35–37)
   (x) <u>will</u> be paid for (lines 38–41)

4. (i) 'No, we won't.' (lines 48–51)
   (ii) 'We will pay for weather damage to inside pipes but not to pipes which are outside.' (lines 46–49)
   (iii) 'We will pay you for any damage for which you are legally responsible.' (lines 53–55)
   (iv) 'Yes, we will.' (lines 57–58)
   (v) 'No, we won't.' (lines 63–65)
   (vi) 'Yes, we will, as long as the requirement is made *after* the earthquake damages your house.' (lines 72–74)
   (vii) 'Yes, we will.' (lines 75–76 and 80–81)
   (viii) 'Yes, it will for up to three months.' (lines 90–93)

Vocabulary

5 (b) (i) incurred
   (ii) civil commotion
   (iii) Reinstating
   (iv) comply
   (v) collision
   (vi) Vandalism
   (vii) heave
   (viii) malicious acts

Text 6.2

Skim and scan

The maximum amount is £1,000,000 (line 32).

Text organisation

1. (i) 4
   (ii) 3
   (iii) 5
   (iv) 6
   (v) 2
   (vi) 1

2. (i) (b) (lines 1–4)
   (ii) (d) (lines 5–8)
   (iii) (a) (lines 9–11)
   (iv) (c) (line 15)

3.

Insurance company must pay	Insurance company need not pay
(ii) (line 21)	(i) (lines 24–28)
(iii) (line 21)	(iv) (lines 24 and 29–30)
(vi) (line 21)	(v) (lines 24 and 29–30)
(vii) (line 22)	(viii) (lines 24 and 29–30)
(ix) (line 21)	

4. (a) (xiii)
   (b) (iv)
   (c) (vi)
   (d) (v)
   (e) (ix)
   (f) (i)
   (g) (viii)
   (h) (i)
   (i) (xi)
   (j) (iii)
   (k) (xv)
   (l) (xiv)
   (m) (x)
   (n) (vii)
   (o) (xii)

Text 6.3

Skim and scan

(a) The company should be told immediately (lines 2–3).

(b) They must give seven days' warning (lines 35–36).

Comprehension

1. (i) False (lines 5–7)
   (ii) True (lines 8–10)
   (iii) True (lines 12–14)
   (iv) False (lines 12 and 15)
   (v) False (lines 18–20)
   (vi) False (lines 21–23)

2. Answers can be expressed in different words from those given here but the meaning must be the same.
   (i) ... will be entitled to benefit under this policy. (lines 24–26)
   (ii) ... take all reasonable steps to prevent loss, damage or accident and maintain the property in a good condition. (lines 27–30)
   (iii) the insurance company will make a refund of premium paid for any period of the insurance that has not been used. (lines 32–34)
   (iv) the insurance company will give seven days' notice that the policy will be cancelled. (lines 38–39)

Vocabulary

3. (i) potential (line 2)
   (ii) give notice (line 3)
   (iii) estimates (line 7)
   (iv) deception (line 8)
   (v) writ (line 13) and summons (line 13)
   (vi) abandoned (line 17)
   (vii) enforce (line 19)
   (viii) proportionate (line 23)
   (ix) entitled (line 25)
   (x) comply with (line 25)
   (xi) maintain (line 30)
   (xii) unexpired (line 33)
   (xiii) ceases (line 38)

Unit 7 Reinsurance

Text 7.1

Skim and scan

(i) Heading C

(ii) Heading A

(iii) Heading B

Text organisation

1. (a) (v) (d) (iv)
   (b) (ii) (e) (iii)
   (c) (i)

Comprehension

2. (i) Statements (d) (lines 13–16), (e) (lines 7–8), (h) (lines 9–14)
   (ii) Statements (d) (lines 38–40), (g) (lines 17–18), (h) (lines 36–37)
   (iii) Statements (a) (lines 41–42), (b) lines 41–42) (c) (lines 42–43), (f) (lines 43–45)

3. (a) Insurance company X will pay 60% of any future loss and reinsurance company Y will pay 40%. (This is assuming that the insurance company assumes the larger share of the loss; otherwise the proportions would be reversed.) (lines 9–12)
   (b) Insurance company X will receive 60% of the premium and reinsurance company Y 20%. (This is assuming that the larger share of any loss is company X's responsibility; otherwise the share of the premium would be reversed.) (lines 12–14)
   (c) Company Y will, in fact, receive less than 40% because X keeps a bit more of the premium for finding the client and administering the policy. (lines 14–16)

4. (a) net retention (lines 27–28)
   (b) 'lines' (lines 28–30)
   (c) The number of 'lines' that a reinsurer accepts is calculated as a multiple of the net retention figure (lines 28–31).

5. (a) Alpha Insurance will pay out $25,000, Beta Reinsurance will pay out $150,000 and Gamma Reinsurance will pay out the remaining amount, i.e. $75,000 (lines 40–58).
   (b) Alpha will get $\frac{\$25,000}{\$250,000} \times 100$
   = 10% of the premium.

   Beta will get $\frac{\$150,000}{\$250,000} \times 100$
   = 60% of the premium.

   Gamma will get $\frac{\$75,000}{\$250,000} \times 100$
   = 30% of the premium.

   It should be noted that Alpha Insurance will receive a bit more than 10% of the premium for arranging the insurance and reinsurance. Beta and Gamma Reinsurance will,therefore, each receive a bit less than their full percentage of the premium. (lines 38–40)

6. A reinsurer in an excess-loss treaty has to (lines 41–42) pay when a loss is greater than an agreed amount. An excess-loss treaty is (lines 42–43) similar to an ordinary insurance policy which has (lines 42–43) a large portion of the loss covered by the initial insurer. An excess-loss treaty can (lines 43–45) cover more than a single risk. There is (lines 41–50) a limit to the liability of the reinsurer with such a treaty.

Vocabulary

7. (i) (m)
   (ii) (a)
   (iii) (k)
   (iv) (n)
   (v) (b)
   (vi) (h)
   (vii) (j)
   (viii) (f)
   (ix) (c)
   (x) (e)
   (xi) (i)
   (xii) (e)
   (xiii) (g)
   (xiv) (d)

Text organisation

8. Still another method of reinsurance is pooling. The pooling arrangement may be similar to that used in aviation insurance under the terms of which each member assumes a percentage of every risk written by a member of the pool. This pooling arrangement is similar to a quota share treaty. On the other hand, the pool may provide a maximum loss limit to any one insurance company from a single loss, as is the case with the Workmens' Compensation Reinsurance Bureau. After a member of the pool has suffered a loss in excess of a specified amount (e.g. £100,000 as a result of one disaster), the other members of the pool share the remainder of the loss.

Text 7.2

Skim and scan

(a) Munich Re and Swiss Re (lines 27–28)
(b) A recent earthquake in Los Angeles (lines 65–66)

Comprehension

1. Summary (c) is the best. (a) has too much detail for a summary. Also it doesn't say enough about the role and functioning of the reinsurance industry. Summary (b) gives too much emphasis to what happened in Florida and not enough to the reinsurance industry as a whole. In summary (d) some of the information is inaccurate. For example, the reinsurance industry wasn't reorganised, Lloyd's is still important etc.

Text organisation

2. (i) As a result
   (ii) if
   (iii) whether
   (iv) notably
   (v) that (with the meaning 'why', as in line 36)
   (vi) hitherto
   (vii) even
   (viii) rather than
   (ix) that (with the meaning 'which', as in line 31)
   (x) As

Comprehension

3. (i) $7 billion (lines 60–63)
   (ii) $15 billion (lines 3–7)
   (iii) $12 billion (lines 45–47)
   (iv) 50%–200% (lines 17–19)

4. (i) Statement (e) (lines 3–7)
   (ii) Statement (e) (lines 3–7)
   (iii) Statement (a) (lines 27–29) and statement (j) (lines 38–41)
   (iv) Statement (a) (lines 27–29)
   (v) Statement (b) (lines 32–35) and statement (j) (lines 54–56)
   (vi) Statement (d) (lines 48–49)
   (vii) Statement (h) (lines 56–63)
   (viii) Statement (i) (lines 66–67)
   (ix) Statement (f) (lines 67–72)
   (x) Statement (c) (lines 72–76)

5. (i) 5 (v) 2
   (ii) 8 (vi) 4
   (iii) 1 (vii) 6
   (iv) 3 (viii) 7

Vocabulary

(i) (h) (vi) (e)
(ii) (g) (vii) (d)
(iii) (b) (viii) (j)
(iv) (i) (ix) (a)
(v) (f) (x) (c)

Unit 8 Risk management and insurance

Text 8.1

Skim and scan

(a) Speculative risks and pure risks (lines 9–10)
(b) Seven (lines 32–33)

Text organisation

1. (i) Paragraph 4
   (ii) Paragraph 3
   (iii) Paragraph 1
   (iv) Paragraph 2
   (v) Paragraph 6
   (vi) Paragraph 5

Comprehension

2. (a), (b) The three steps, in the correct order, are (v), (iv) and (ii).

3. (i) PR (line 17)
   (ii) PR (lines 17–23)
   (iii) SR (lines 11–14)
   (iv) SR (lines 10–11)
   (v) SR (lines 11–14)
   (vi) PR (lines 17– 21)
   (vii) SR (lines 15–16) This is rather an exceptional speculative risk because steps can be taken to guard against it, i.e. hedging (line 16).
   (viii) PR (line 22)

4. (i) (e) (v) (f)
   (ii) (c) (vi) (d)
   (iii) (g) (vii) (b)
   (iv) (a)

5. (a) (iii) (lines 40–42)
   (b) (i) (lines 45–47)

6. Risk management method A: Insurance (lines 49–50)
   Main points:
   (i) The correct amount of insurance providing the right services must be purchased at the lowest cost (lines 50–52).
   (ii) The rules of the insurance policy must be carefully obeyed (lines 52–55).

Risk management method B: Loss prevention (line 56)
Main points:
- (i) The employees must be aware of the program and understand their role in it (lines 56–58).
- (ii) The risk manager must be aware of all advances in safety methods (lines 58–60).

Vocabulary

7. (i) (c)
   (ii) (g)
   (iii) (a)
   (iv) (i)
   (v) (k)
   (vi) (n)
   (vii) (h)
   (viii) (b)
   (ix) (m)
   (x) (d)
   (xi) (l)
   (xii) (e)
   (xiii) (f)
   (xiv) (j)

Text organisation

8. (i) 4
   (ii) 1
   (iii) 6
   (iv) 2
   (v) 5
   (vi) 3

Text 8.2

Skim and scan

- (a) They came from an insurance background (lines 2–3)
- (b) No (line 9)

Text organisation

1. (i) (d)
   (ii) (i)
   (iii) (j)
   (iv) (e)
   (v) (a)
   (vi) (k)
   (vii) (h)
   (viii) (g)
   (ix) (c)
   (x) (l)
   (xi) (f)
   (xii) (b)

Comprehension

2. (a) One of risk management's main problems has been to show how it is different from insurance (lines 1–2).
   (b) (i) Many people who developed risk management had worked in insurance before (lines 2–3).
   (ii) Risk has for a long time been thought to be connected with insurance only (lines 3–6).
   (iii) Insurance is still a very important part of any risk management program (lines 6–8).

3. (i) x (line 9)
   (ii) ✓ (lines 9–11)
   (iii) ✓ (lines 11–13)
   (iv) x (lines 13–14)

4. (i) 3 (line 18)
   (ii) 1 (lines 15–16)
   (iii) 4 (lines 18–19)
   (iv) 2 (lines 16–17)

5. (i) False (lined 20–21)
   (ii) True (lines 26–28)
   (iii) True (lines 28–30)
   (iv) True (lines 30–31)
   (v) False (lines 30–33)
   (vi) False (lines 34–35)
   (vii) True (lines 34–37)
   (viii) False (lines 41–43)

6. (a) Risk spreading (lines 44–46)
   (b) Two types (lines 46–53)
   (c) (i) Insuring a lot of the same type of risk (lines 46–48)
   (ii) Making sure that the risks being insured come from many different places (lines 50–53)

Vocabulary

7. (a) (i) overcome (line 1)
   (ii) the preserve of (line 5)
   (iii) retains (line 6)
   (iv) breach (line 18)
   (v) subsequent (line 23)
   (vi) governed (line 26)
   (vii) defer (line 27)
   (viii) chronological (line 34)
   (ix) thereby (line 35)
   (x) synonymous (line 42)

(b) (i) endeavour
(ii) differentiate
(iii) superseded
(iv) minimise
(v) is perpetuated

Text organisation

8. (i) 3
(ii) 1
(iii) 2

Unit 9 Insurance organisations

Text 9.1

Skim and scan

(a) *Allfinanz* is 'the marriage of banking with insurance and other services for retail customers' (lines 1–3).
(b) It bought Deutscher Herold (lines 70–73)

Text organisation

1. (i) Paragraph 2
(ii) Paragraph 6
(iii) Paragraph 3
(iv) Paragraph 1
(v) Paragraph 7
(vi) Paragraph 5
(vii) Paragraph 4

Comprehension

2. (a) The Germans did (line 1).
(b) This is ironic because the movement towards *Allfinanz* is less advanced in Germany than in some other European countries (lines 3–7.)
(c) The situation in 2(b) could change because of the deregulation of Germany's insurance market in 1994 (lines 7–12).

3. (a) Four reasons are given in the text (lines 15–24).
(b) (i) (lines 18–21), (iv) (lines 21–24), (vi) (lines 15–16), (viii) (lines 16–18)

4. No, the author doesn't think such alliances are a good idea. Lines 25–27 show this.

5. (i) Statements (j) (lines 27–31), (g) (lines 31–32) and (k) (lines 34–36)
(ii) Statements (d) (lines 34–35) and (a) (lines 34–36)
(iii) Statements (i) (lines 38–39), (f) (lines 40–41) and (h) (lines 41–42)
(iv) Statements (c) (lines 38–40), (e) (lines 42–43) and (b) (lines 44–45)

6. (a) Germany's insurance market was deregulated (lines 46–47).
(b) This deregulation should free prices and permit insurers to try new products (lines 47–48).
(c) These freer prices and new products would cause banks and insurers to come together more closely in different kinds of relationships. (lines 48–51)

7. (i) False (lines 51–53)
(ii) True (lines 53–54)
(iii) False (lines 57–59)
(iv) True (lines 59–60)
(v) False (lines 60–63)

8. (i) 4 (lines 73–75)
(ii) 2 (lines 67–69)
(iii) 3 (lines 70–73)
(iv) 1 (lines 66–67)

Vocabulary

9. (ii) I developed more slowly
(iii) I insignificant
(iv) F delay
(v) I connected
(vi) F not wanting
(vii) F in case
(viii) F requires
(ix) F small
(x) I suddenly entered
(xi) I compel
(xii) I intensifies
(xiii) I disagreeing
(xiv) I divide
(xv) F gives up

Text 9.2

Skim and scan

(a) The new chairman of Lloyd's (lines 21–22)
(b) An 'independent consultancy' (lines 42–43)

Text organisation

1. (i) Paragraph 3
 (ii) Paragraph 6
 (iii) Paragraph 1
 (iv) Paragraph 4
 (v) Paragraph 2
 (vi) Paragraph 5

2. (ii) 'This' in line 4
 (iii) 'this collection of co-operatives' in line 9
 (iv) 'this thought' in line 15
 (v) 'its' in line 17
 (vi) 'its' and 'it' in lines 19 and 20
 (vii) 'that' in line 28
 (viii) 'That' in line 34
 (ix) 'these disasters' in line 40
 (x) 'they' (twice) in line 50
 (xi) 'many' in line 64

Comprehension

3. (i) 2 late '70s, and early '80s (lines 17–18)
 (ii) 9 ('the next couple of years', line 24)
 (iii) 3 1983 (lines 27–28)
 (iv) 8 1991 ('today', line 29; i.e. when this article was written)
 (v) 5 1987 (lines 30–31)
 (vi) 4 1986 (lines 33–34)
 (vii) 7 1988–90 (lines 34–35)
 (viii) 1 1967 (line 45)
 (ix) 6 1987–89 (lines 66–68)

4. (a) (iv) (lines 11–14)
 (b) (ii) (lines 23–27)

5. (a) After three years (lines 31–33)
 (b) 32,500 (lines 46–49)

6. It is not possible for a Lloyd's account to be closed when there are still claims against it which have not been settled (lines 51–54)

7. (a) (vi) (lines 61–63)
 (b) (ii) (lines 50–53)
 (c) (i) (lines 64–68)
 (d) (iii) (lines 61–63)
 (e) (v) (line 51)
 (f) (iv) (line 55)

8. (a) 'long-tail' claims (line 70)
 (b) the bad management of American savings-and-loan institutions in the 1980s (lines 72–75)

Vocabulary

9. (a) (i) earn
 (ii) improve
 (iii) be in a trap
 (iv) increase
 (b) (i) There was a lot of dishonest business activity going on at Lloyd's at this time.
 (ii) Absolutely clean, without even the smallest trace of dishonesty.
 (iii) Something connected with asbestos, in this case insurance risks.
 (c) (i) 'putting Lloyd's … under its thumb' (lines 16–17), meaning B
 (ii) 'shaken the dust of Lloyd's from their feet' (line 48), meaning C
 (iii) 'Open years are proving to be open wounds' (lines 75–76), meaning A
 (d) (i) bleak
 (ii) pledged
 (iii) enfeeble
 (iv) underscored
 (v) meagre
 (vi) spate
 (vii) singular
 (viii) scions
 (ix) Spillage
 (x) notoriety
 (xi) Notable
 (xii) haunted by
 (xiii) synonymous with

Unit 10 Insurance marketing

Text 10.1

Skim and scan

(a) The *Yellow Pages* and *Dun & Bradstreet* (line 10)
(b) $238,000 (lines 55–56)

Text organisation

1. (c) is the best summary. (a) doesn't mention the second mathematical model at all and this is a very important part of the text. (b) has too much detail to be a good summary. (d) has some information which is not correct according to the text; e.g. United sells only to self-employed persons, its agents also sell other insurance companies, etc.

2. (ii) 'themselves' in line 4
(iii) 'such leads' in line 7
(iv) 'these lists' in line 12
(v) 'such sources' in line 10
(vi) 'it' in line 16
(vii) 'they' in line 21
(viii) 'This model' in line 27
(ix) 'This second model' in line 45
(x) 'this test' in line 48 and 'this test' in line 54
(xi) 'their' in line 46
(xii) 'this model' in line 56
(xiii) 'it' in line 55

Comprehension

3. (i) True (lines 2–4)
(ii) True (line 5)
(iii) False – they 'rely on a one-call close' (lines 5–6).
(iv) False – United has 1000 agents (line 6).
(v) True – 25,000,000 mailings and phone calls produce 750,000 leads = 33 mailings and calls per lead (lines 6–9).

4. (i) (b) (lines 19–19)
(ii) (g) (lines 19–20)
(iii) (e) (lines 19 and 21–22)
(iv) (f) (lines 21–22)
(v) (d) (lines 23–24)
(vi) (a) (lines 23–25)
(vii) (c) (lines 25–26)

5. (a) (ii) (lines 28–31)
(b) An individual number was given to each consumer factor which was thought to be linked to the premiums bought by each group of consumers. These were then added together to produce a total. (lines 32–36)
(c) The best potential customer was given a score of 1000 and the worst potential customer a score of zero.

6. (i) 268 (line 39 and line 42)
(ii) 107 (lines 38 and 41)
(iii) 56 (line 38 and line 41)
(iv) 171 (line 38 and lines 41–42)

7. (i) 4 (lines 45–46)
(ii) 1 (lines 43–44)
(iii) 3 (lines 46–47)
(iv) 2 (lines 44–45)

8. (a) Businesses with score values of 350 or more (lines 50–51)
(b) Businesses with score values of 225 or more (lines 52–53)
(c) Leads (lines 51 and 53)
(d) Businesses with score values of 225 or more (lines 52–53)
(e) Businesses with score values of 350 or more (lines 50–51)
(f) Sales (lines 51–52 and 52–53)
(g) 97% (line 53)
(h) 26% (lines 51–52)

9. (a) United decided in the future to send mailings only to companies which had a score value of 225 or more (lines 54–55)
(b) United thinks that this decision will save them $238,000 a year in postal costs (lines 55–56)

Vocabulary

10. (i) exclusively (line 5)
(ii) leads (line 7)
(iii) generated (line 7)
(iv) responsive (line 11)
(v) criteria (line 13)
(vi) lapses (line 14)

(vii)	yielded	(line 21)
(viii)	refined	(line 28)
(ix)	evaluated	(line 28)
(x)	traits	(line 33)
(xi)	assigned	(line 35)
(xii)	accounted	(line 50)
(xiii)	restrict	(line 54)

Text 10.2

Skim and scan

(a) Annuities are contracts by which an investor is periodically paid an amount of money in return for an initial single investment (lines 46–48)

(b) Banking products (lines 56–59)

Comprehension

1. (i) False (lines 6–13)
   (ii) True (lines 17–24)
   (iii) True (lines 17–21)
   (iv) False (lines 24–28)

2. (i) Supported (lines 33–36)
   (ii) Opposed (lines 45–51)
   (iii) Supported (lines 51–58)
   (iv) Supported (lines 56–59)

3. (i) (c) (lines 33–36)
   (ii) (a) (lines 45–49)
   (iii) (b) (lines 51–59)

4. (a) No, they are not unusual.
   (b) The other type of common legal conflict is that between federal and state law.
   (c) Lines 60–65.

5 The Owenboro National Bank has been in conflict with Kentucky <u>insurance</u> (lines 69–71) regulations about whether it can sell insurance products <u>in Kentucky</u> (lines 71–72). Tom Brumley, the president, <u>has</u> (lines 74–77) a client base to whom his bank can sell insurance. <u>Kentucky</u> (lines 78–79) law prevents staff of banks selling insurance although <u>national</u> (lines 81–82) law allows it. The question of which law has priority will be decided by a <u>federal</u> (lines 79–81) appeals court.

6. (a) It said banks could sell insurance <u>from</u> small towns (lines 87–89)
   (b) It seemed to say that banks could only sell insurance <u>in</u> small towns (lines 94–96)
   (c) The Washington decision would be better for them because they want to market insurance products nationally (lines 89–94)

7. (a) The problems will probably be sorted out in the courts, most likely the supreme court (lines 97–99).
   (b) This will probably be the case because banking and insurance groups ('vested interest', line 99) would stop any legislation in the US Congress that they did not like (lines 100–103)

Vocabulary

8.

(i)	wedged	(line 6)
(ii)	convoluted	(line 9)
(iii)	loophole	(line 18)
(iv)	flurry	(line 29)
(v)	setback	(line 38)
(vi)	runs counter to	(lines 51–52)
(vii)	arm	(line 54)
(viii)	adhere to	(line 59)
(ix)	discrepancies	(line 62)
(x)	litigation	(line 65)
(xi)	Echoing	(line 73)
(xii)	comprise	(line 76)
(xiii)	primacy over	(line 82)
(xiv)	ironed out	(line 98)
(xv)	vested interest	(line 99)

Text organisation

9. The complete summary should be as follows:

A small town in America, Banks, Oregon, is at the centre of legal battles about whether banks should be allowed to sell insurance. American law apparently permits nationally regulated banks to market insurance from towns with populations under 5,000. Insurance agents, wanting to protect their own business, have taken legal action against banks which have tried to use this law. A federal court in Washington originally supported the banks' position but a recent legal decision could change this situation. In this case it was ruled that annuities were an insurance product and not a banking one as the US Treasury claims. Such legal disputes are not new, however, as is shown by the situation of a Kentucky bank which has been trying to sell insurance products for three years. Here the dispute is over whether Kentucky state law, which forbids banks selling insurance, has priority over federal law, which allows it. The problem is further complicated in that it is not clear if banks can only sell insurance in towns with less than 5,000 people or also from them. It seems likely that the whole question will have to be decided in the American Supreme Court rather than by new legislation.

Glossary

This glossary explains how the words are used in this book, although they may have other meanings. Apart from these words, the meanings of many other specialised insurance terms are explained in the texts or by doing the exercises.

Actuarial tables Results of mathematical calculations which show the probability of a risk affecting a particular type of insurance. The calculations are done by actuaries.

Bonds A formal document promising to pay an amount of money or confirming that a debt exists.

Budget The occasion when the British Chancellor of the Exchequer states how much money the government intends to raise and spend in the next year.

Building societies British financial institutions that take deposits and loan those for home-buying.

City of London The area in London where many important financial institutions are located.

Commission A form of payment based on how much a sales representative sells or how much business an agent provides a client.

Commodities Certain basic substances, such as wheat and raw cotton, which need processing before they can be consumed.

Corporation (US) A large company whose shares can usually be bought on a stock exchange.

Direct writers Those insurers that sell insurance directly to clients without using an intermediary, i.e. an insurance broker.

Direct writing company An insurance company that sells insurance directly to customers without using a broker.

Disabled People who suffer from some physical handicap such as blindness or loss of a leg.

Executive A high-level manager in a company.

GDR German Democratic Republic. Former name for East Germany before it became part of the German Federal Republic.

General Agreement on Tariffs and Trade (GATT) International commercial treaty aimed at reducing the level of taxes on imports to encourage world trade.

Insured(s) A person or organisation which is covered by a particular insurance policy.

Law of Large Numbers This mathematical rule states that in the long term the percentage of times that something actually happens becomes closer to the predicted percentage that it will happen.

Lead generation The process of getting the names of potential customers.

Local authority The institution which is responsible for providing local government.

Mortgage A loan provided by a bank or building society so that property can be purchased.

Names The private individuals who back the insurance policies written at Lloyd's of London by committing their wealth on a basis of unlimited liability.

No-claim bonuses The reduction in the cost of insurance which is given to those people who have not made a claim against a policy.

NHS The National Health Service. The system of mainly free health care provided by the British state for its citizens.

OECD The Organisation for Economic Co-operation and Development.

One-call close The sales method which involves trying to make a sale on the basis of only one telephone call or visit.

Policy holder A person who is covered by some kind of insurance policy.

Profit-sharing A system by which any profits made are divided between those individuals or organisations who are responsible for making that profit.

Real estate (US) Property which is being bought or sold.

Risk-pooling plan A fundamental concept of insurance where a number of individuals or organisations all pay money into a fund which is used to pay any specified losses suffered by a few of them.

Securities A general name given to stock exchange investments, e.g. company shares and bonds.

Social Security The system where the government provides support for those most in need, e.g. unemployment pay for those without a job.

Statute A written law.

Stock Exchange The institution in a country where the shares of companies can be bought and sold.

Stock A word often used instead of 'share', i.e. an investment in a company involving some legal claim on that company.

Supreme Court The highest court in America which makes the final decision regarding any legal dispute.

Tax exemptions Certain allowances which mean that tax need not be paid.

Trade union An organisation in which workers join together to improve their wages and working conditions.

Trust fund Economic assets which are administered by trustees for the benefit of others.

Trustees Persons who administer funds, property or some other form of wealth for the benefit of others.

Underwriting syndicates A group of Lloyd's underwriters (i.e. those who accept insurance risks and decide premiums to insure those risks) working together as a group.